A Creative Approach to the Classical Progymnasmata

Writing Rhetoric

Book 2: Narrative I

Paul Kortepeter

Writing & Rhetoric Book 2: Narrative I
© Classical Academic Press, 2013
Version 2.0

ISBN: 978-1-60051-218-6

Classical Academic Press
515 S. 32nd Street
Camp Hill, PA 17011

www.ClassicalAcademicPress.com

Series content editor: Christine Perrin
Series editor: Gretchen Nesbit
Illustrations: Jason Rayner
Book design: Karen Brightbill
p. 48: Photograph of *The Blindman and the Lame* statue by Jean Turcan
used courtesy of Rama, Wikimedia Commons, Cc-by-sa-2.0-fr.
p. 84: Image of statue of Leonidas used courtesy of Neoptolemus and Selre4ok
under the GNU Free Documentation License.

PGP.03.19

Narrative I

TABLE OF CONTENTS

A Typical Teaching Week v
Introduction to Students vi
Introduction

Writing Happily viii
Best Foot Forward   The *Progym* and the Practice of Modern Writing xii
                                  Objectives for *Narrative I* xii

Lesson 1: *All Kinds of Stories* 1

Lesson 2: *A Long Parable* 10
The Prodigal Son

Lesson 3: *A Short Parable* 28
The Rich Fool

Lesson 4: *Main Idea—Parables* 41
The Lame Man and the Blind Man
The Crying Woman

Lesson 5: *Dialogue—A Greek Myth* 47
Athena Defeats Poseidon

Lesson 6: *Description—Another Greek Myth* 62
Athena and Arachne

Lesson 7: *Combining Dialogue and Description, Part I* 75
The Brave 300

Lesson 8: Combining Dialogue and Description, Part 2 86
Romulus and Remus

Lesson 9: Conflict—The Middle of the Story 101
Alexander and Bucephalus

Lesson 10: More Practice with Story Middles 117
The Johnny-Cake
The Sausage
Samba the Coward

Elocution Instructions 129

Glossary of Words in This Book 130

Another Good-bye 131

A Typical Teaching Week

Veteran teachers know that rarely is there anything typical about a teaching week. These guidelines are intended to help bring some predictability to lesson planning. Although the parts of speech and other elements of grammar are important aspects of this course, its primary focus is writing and rhetoric—as the name implies. It is recommended that teachers alternate between a course in grammar one week and *Writing & Rhetoric: Narrative I* the next week. The schedule includes four days so that you can have flexibility to spend more time on some sections or to catch up.

Day One

1. The teacher models fluency by reading the text aloud while students follow along silently.

2. Students break off into pairs and reread the text to each other. In the case of longer fables, students can read in sections. Encouragement should be given to students to read with drama and flair where appropriate.

3. "Tell It Back" (Narration) and "Talk About It" should immediately follow the reading of the text, while the fable is still fresh in the students' minds. "Talk About It" is designed to help students analyze the meaning of texts and to see analogous situations, both in the world and in their own lives. Narration, the process of "telling back," can be done in pairs or by selecting individuals to narrate to the entire class. Playacting the story from memory is another possible form of narration. (Note: Solo students can tell back the story into a recording device or to an instructor.) The process of narration is intended to improve comprehension and long-term memory.

4. "Go Deeper" comprehension exercises follow each text. They can help students better understand the selection as they work with vocabulary, main ideas, and character traits.

Day Two

1. Optional: The teacher can appoint a student or the entire class to read the text again.

2. Students then work with the text through the "Writing Time" exercises. In ancient times, at this level, the primary exercise was to summarize or amplify the length of the narrative. Other exercises include emulating a particular sentence, changing part of a story, or writing an entirely new story. Student work need not be completely original, but it should show some effort of thought.

Day Three or Four*

1. A time of sharing work can wrap up each lesson. In order to build confidence in public speaking, students should be encouraged to read their work aloud—either in pairs or to the entire class.

2. The "Speak It" section creates opportunities for students to recite, to play act, and to share their work aloud. Please consider using a recording device whenever it would suit the situation. In this case, have the student listen back to her recording to get an idea of what sounded right and what could be improved. Have students read the elocution instructions at the end of the book to help them work on skill in presentation.

*The number of days per week assigned to the lessons is four so that you have some flexibility according to the pace and level of depth that you can take advantage of with your students.

Introduction to Students

We are glad you are studying writing and rhetoric and we think you will be glad, too! In the Writing & Rhetoric series, we use whole stories to teach you how to write. First you read and think about the stories, then you have the chance to rewrite them, making them longer or shorter. Eventually, after you learn how to do that, you will write your own story. By that time, your mind will be filled with characters, words, events, and even types of sentences that will help you write.

Often, when people are taught to write, they are asked to come up with material from thin air, or *ex nihilo*, which is a Latin phrase that means "out of nothing." For instance, many students return to school in the fall and are asked to write about their summer vacation. This can be fun, but we believe the best writing skills are developed when you have many ideas, words, and examples that show you a lot of ways in which other writers have written about a subject. In a way, these other writers become your writing guides. Frequently, when a writer doesn't have such a guide, he or she gets frustrated. Even famous writers have had such guides—often their work resembles the writing style of their teachers or guides.

Now, let's get writing!

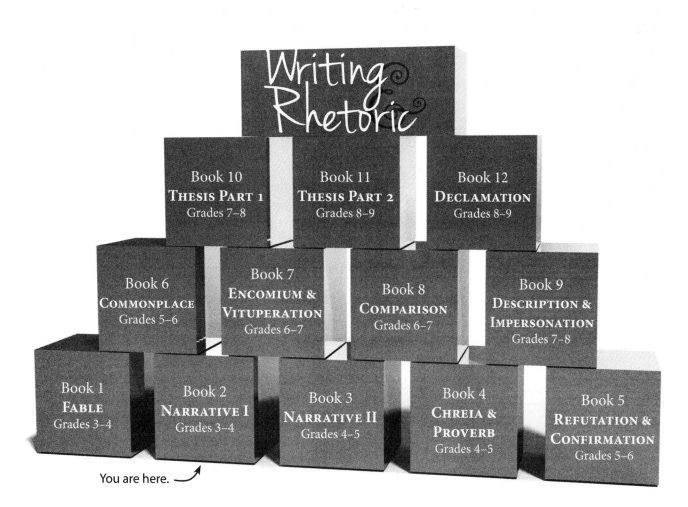

Writing & Rhetoric

Book 10
THESIS PART 1
Grades 7–8

Book 11
THESIS PART 2
Grades 8–9

Book 12
DECLAMATION
Grades 8–9

Book 6
COMMONPLACE
Grades 5–6

Book 7
**ENCOMIUM &
VITUPERATION**
Grades 6–7

Book 8
COMPARISON
Grades 6–7

Book 9
**DESCRIPTION &
IMPERSONATION**
Grades 7–8

Book 1
FABLE
Grades 3–4

Book 2
NARRATIVE I
Grades 3–4

Book 3
NARRATIVE II
Grades 4–5

Book 4
**CHREIA &
PROVERB**
Grades 4–5

Book 5
**REFUTATION &
CONFIRMATION**
Grades 5–6

You are here.

The Writing & Rhetoric series provides students with forms and models of excellent writing that students can imitate on their path to masterful writing. The second book in the series continues the recovery of this proven method of teaching writing, using various forms of narrative to teach beginning writers the craft of writing well.

This is the second in a series of twelve books that will train students over six years, starting in grades three or four and up.

Introduction

Writing Happily

Where We Are Now with Writing

When it comes to writing, some students see the process as sweet delight. That was my experience. I always loved taking a blank sheet of paper and transforming it into something magical: a carnival twinkling in the night, a city street shining with rain and reflecting gas lamps, an avalanche flying down a spire of rock. But I know that writing is not a magical world for many children or even some adults.

When I served as a writing instructor at the University of Southern California (USC), I saw first-hand the failure of writing instruction at our primary and secondary schools. Hardly a day went by that I wasn't grading a stack of papers, and the torment, the agony, of writing seemed to writhe through the pages.

Many of those college students had difficulty writing grammatically correct and coherent paragraphs—let alone entire essays, persuasively written. These were smart students from privileged backgrounds. So how did they get to college with such meager writing skills? What was happening in school or at home to sabotage the development of writing? Something was clearly not working.

Some years after teaching at USC, I helped to establish The Oaks Academy in the inner city of Indianapolis. Our school has grown from a modest fifty students in 1998 to 500-plus students today. At The Oaks, our mission is "to provide a rich, classical education to children of diverse racial and socioeconomic backgrounds." Our diversity includes children who grow up in highly involved families as well as children who have limited access to opportunity and must often fend for themselves academically.

As director of curriculum, I was determined to find a writing program that served the needs of all of our students. I wanted a program that combined the best modern practices with the principles of classical education as defined by such disparate educators as the Roman rhetorician Quintilian and nineteenth-century British reformer Charlotte Mason. I felt strongly that students could be confident, persuasive writers by the eighth grade if they received the right combination of models and practice. Above all, I wanted to avoid the wasted years that led to faltering communication in college and beyond.

I examined quite a few programs. Each in its own way seemed to be lacking—both the modern courses and those purporting to be classically inspired. Nothing seemed to be "just right." Some programs were difficult to use. Others seemed too frivolous on the one hand or too heavy on the other. Still others lacked the necessary incremental steps.

The book you have in your hand is the fruit of my dissatisfaction. This is a curriculum built on the solid foundations of the past and framed with the vitality of the present. This is a curriculum that has been tested by ancient, medieval, and modern kids, and proven reliable for the ages. Along with caring teachers and a diet of good books, The Writing & Rhetoric series has taken the young people of The Oaks, kids from all sorts of advantaged and disadvantaged backgrounds, and shaped them into fine communicators. As a current eighth-grade teacher, I am often delighted by the rhetorical firepower in my classroom.

Imitation as a Foundation for Learning Writing

An examination of the theory and practice of modern composition reveals some obvious problems. Too often students are asked to brainstorm, "prewrite," or "freewrite" according to their personal interests. This means, in essence, that they are supposed to conjure ideas out of thin air. When faced with a blank piece of paper, many students naturally draw a blank. They lack a conversation in their heads about where to begin. Good writing requires content. It abhors a vacuum.

Students are also expected to write with no clear model before them. Modern composition scolds traditional writing instruction as rote and unimaginative. It takes imitation to task for a lack of freedom and personal expression. And yet effective communication from writer to reader always requires some sort of form and structure. Many of history's greatest writers learned by imitation. Benjamin Franklin, for example, taught himself to write by studying classic books and copying whole passages verbatim. He would then put the book aside and try to reconstruct the passage from memory.

Today's emphasis on originality and creativity has failed. When students lack a form by which to express their ideas, their creativity lacks vitality. As Alexander Pope tells us in his "An Essay on Criticism": "True Ease in Writing comes from Art, not Chance, / As those move easiest who have learn'd to dance." In other words, writing takes the same kind of determined study as ballet or diving. Creativity uses conventional form as a stage or a springboard from which to launch grand *jetés* and somersaults.

But there's yet another problem. Too often students are expected to tackle complex writing assignments without learning the necessary intermediate steps. Without due concern, teachers require summer vacation narratives, persuasive letters, research papers, and poetic descriptions. All of these forms require skills that must be developed in stages. The assumption is that because most everyone can speak English well enough to be understood, and form letters with a pencil, that everyone should be able to write well. And yet how many of us would expect a child to sit at a piano, without piano lessons, and play a concerto? How many of us would expect a child with a hammer and a chisel and a block of marble to carve the statue of David as well as Michelangelo?

Writing is never automatic. The skills of the trade will not miraculously materialize somewhere along the school way. They take years to master. This is because writing demands thoughtfulness, organization, grammatical skill, rhetorical skill, and an ear for the English language. Most children have a natural inclination for one or two of these skills. Rarely do they have a knack for all. The other skills need to be developed and matured.

When it comes down to it, writing is simply thinking on paper. Or thinking in some digital realm. Writing is thought translated to symbols—the symbolic language of the alphabet. The difficulty lies in the process of translation. I may picture a face or a waterfall clearly in my mind. It's quite another thing to describe the face or waterfall articulately in writing. I may have beautiful arguments on the tip of my tongue for buying a Great Dane puppy, but can I make the case persuasively on a piece of paper? The thinking comes first; the writing comes second. Both need to mature together.

What Is to Be Done

If we have lost our way, it rarely helps to plunge blindly forward. It often helps to retrace our steps. And so it is with writing. We have much to learn from the wisdom of the ages. The Greeks developed a system of persuasive speaking known as rhetoric. The Romans, who came later, were also in love with rhetoric, but they took it to the next level. In order to prepare their young students for dazzling oration, the Romans invented a complementary system of persuasive writing.

This writing system was so dynamic, so effective, that it outlasted the Roman Empire, the Middle Ages, and the Renaissance. It even survived into early modern times. This method employed fluent reading, careful listening, models for imitation, and progressive steps. In short, it did many of the things that are out of fashion today, but gave us writers like Cicero and John Milton.

The Romans in the Greek-speaking part of the Empire called their system the *progymnasmata* (pro-gym-naz-ma-ta). This strange, mouthful of a word derives from the same root for exercise as do "gymnasium" and "gymnastics." It means "preliminary exercises." The goal of these lessons is to prepare students for rhetoric, which is the art of writing well and speaking persuasively. This method assumes that students learn best by reading excellent examples of literature and by growing their skills through imitation. Successful writers study great writing. Successful orators study great speeches.

Each exercise is intended to impart a skill (or tool) that can be employed in all kinds of writing and speaking. The exercises are arranged from simple to more complex. What's more, the exercises are cumulative, meaning that later exercises incorporate the skills acquired in preceding exercises. This means, for example, that the skill of reporting or narrating (derived from the narrative exercise) will be regularly practiced and used in future exercises. While engaging in praising an individual (encomium exercise), a student will need to report or narrate an important event or achievement. While comparing two individuals (comparison exercise), a student will often need to praise an individual (encomium).

Studying and acquiring the skills imparted by the *progymnasmata* (hereafter referred to as *progym*) exercises is much like the way in which we acquire skill in cooking or in a sport such as soccer. In the case of cooking, students must first learn the foundational skills of measuring, pouring, and mixing. Then they must learn skills relating to using a frying pan and oven. Each recipe requires the employment of these foundational skills—no matter how complicated it is. A sport like soccer also requires the mastery of basic skills such as kicking, passing, and dribbling. These foundational skills are carried forward into every soccer play and every game strategy.

Think of the *progym* as a step-by-step apprenticeship in the art of writing and rhetoric. What is an apprentice? It is a young person who is learning a skill from a master teacher. Our students will serve as apprentices to the great writers and great stories of history.

Quintilian, one of the master teachers of Rome, tells us that good habits are the foundation of education. In his *Institutio Oratoria*, he writes, "Once a bad habit has become ingrained, it is easier to break than bend. So strong is custom formed in early years." This master teacher also tells us that natural ability is nothing if it is not "cultivated by skillful teaching, persistent study, and continuous and extensive practice in writing, reading, and speaking."

Getting Started

The place to begin is reading, which should be encouraged as one of life's great pleasures from a child's earliest days. Parents should introduce books to babies as soon as they can keep their eyes open. Babies love to hear the sound of their parents' voices. They love the feeling of snuggling in a parent's lap. They love bright books and pictures. Reading helps develop joint attention, which is necessary for any language acquisition. The more a child reads and is read to, the better the foundation for writing. And if a parent feels he or she has been negligent in reading, it's never too late to get started.

The necessary corollary is that we must limit screens: TV, the Internet, and video games should stay off as much as possible! Without realizing it, many parents sabotage the ability of their children to think by allowing an excess of these media. Researchers are telling us, in no uncertain terms, that an imbalance of electronics can be harmful to clear thinking and focused attention. If children don't have time for books, they don't have time for glowing screens. (Unless, of course, that glowing screen contains a book.) Even boredom and daydreaming can be more productive than too much media exposure! A brain needs rest in order to do the hard work of synthesizing information, problem solving, and making connections between ideas.

Next to reading, it's important for children to get comfortable with the formation of letters. Children should work on penmanship to strengthen neural pathways that allow thinking and writing at the same time. Once writing mechanics come easily, it is much easier to make progress in the complex skill of "thinking on paper." As is often the case, there's more to a fine motor skill than meets the eye. With writing, children must learn to grip the pencil properly, to move their arms and wrists smoothly, and to stay focused on the page. Keep practice sessions short, but frequent—about ten minutes a day for seven- and eight-year-olds.

Before children begin *Writing & Rhetoric: Narrative I*, they should also know how to identify and create a complete sentence. In other words, they should be able to recognize the presence or absence of a subject or a predicate, and know how to use capital letters and simple punctuation. The sentence is the DNA of written ideas. *Writing & Rhetoric: Fable* is the best way to begin this series.

After This—Formal Rhetoric

The formal study of rhetoric will develop in students a solid theoretical understanding of rhetoric, helping them to better understand why and how to employ the skills they have acquired while studying these exercises. The *progym* will prepare your students to enjoy transforming that blank sheet of paper into a spectacular view from atop the pinnacle of their own imagination.

Best Foot Forward

The *Progym* and the Practice of Modern Writing

Although the *progym* are an ancient method of approaching writing, they are extraordinarily relevant today. This is because modern composition owes almost everything to the *progym*. Modern writing borrows heavily from many of the *progym's* various exercises. For example, modern stories are essentially unchanged from the ancient fable and narrative forms. Modern expository essays contain elements from the ancient *chreia*, the refutation/confirmation, and other *progym* exercises. Persuasive essays of today are basically the same as the ancient commonplace and thesis exercises. In this series, you can expect your students to grow in all forms of modern composition—narrative, expository, descriptive, and persuasive—while at the same time developing unique rhetorical muscle.

The *progym* cover a host of the new Common Core Standards for English and the Language Arts. In *Narrative I*, these include:

- Asking and answering questions to demonstrate understanding of the text
- Recounting stories and fables from diverse cultures
- Describing characters in a story
- Determining the meaning of words and phrases in the text
- Distinguishing one's point of view from the point of view of story characters
- Explaining how an illustration enhances the text
- Providing reasons to support an opinion
- Writing narratives to develop imagined experiences

While the goals of the Common Core Standards are certainly worthwhile, the *progym* derive their strength from the incremental and thorough development of each form of writing. The Writing & Rhetoric series does not skip from form to form and leave the others behind, but rather builds a solid foundation of mastery by blending the forms. For example, no expository essay can truly be effective without description. No persuasive essay can be convincing without narrative. All good narrative writing requires description and all good persuasive writing requires expository elements. Not only do the *progym* demand strong organization, but they retain all of the power of classical rhetoric.

Here is how the progym develops each stage of modern composition:

1. Fable—Narrative

2. Narrative—Narrative with descriptive elements

3. *Chreia* & Proverb—Expository essay with narrative, descriptive, and persuasive elements

4. Refutation & Confirmation—Persuasive essay with narrative, descriptive, and expository elements

5. Commonplace—Persuasive essay with narrative, descriptive, and expository elements

6. Encomium & Vituperation—Persuasive essay with narrative, descriptive, and expository elements

7. Comparison—Comparative essay with narrative, descriptive, and expository elements

8. Description & Impersonation—Descriptive essays with narrative, expository, persuasive, and comparative elements

9. Thesis Part 1—Persuasive essay with narrative, descriptive, expository, and comparative elements

10. Thesis Part 2—Persuasive speech with narrative, descriptive, expository, and comparative elements, as well as the three rhetorical appeals

11. Declamation—Persuasive essay or speech that marshals all the elements of the *progym* and brings them to bear upon judicial matters

As you can see, the *progym* move quickly to establish the importance of one form to another.

Objectives for *Narrative I*

Here are some of the major objectives for the exercises found in each section of this book:

1. Expose students to different forms of narrative writing as well as culturally important examples.

2. Model fluent reading for students and give them practice reading short texts.

3. Give students practice in copying texts accurately.

4. Strengthen working memory through dictation, thus improving storage and manipulation of information.

5. Increase understanding of the flexibility and copiousness of language through sentence manipulation.

6. Facilitate student interaction with well-written texts through question and answer and through exercises in summary and amplification.

7. Give students opportunities to creatively imitate sentences and narrative sections.

8. Introduce the concepts of plot (beginning, middle, and end), dialogue, and description.

Lesson 1 ·······································

All Kinds of Stories

Narrative is a fancy word for "story." Your teacher has probably already asked you many times "to narrate" the stories you read in class. "To narrate" means "to tell," and it comes from the Latin word *narrare*, which also means "to tell." So if you are asked to narrate a **narrative**,[1] you are being asked to tell a story.

What would life be like without stories? Without stories, our lives would be as empty and dull as a dark cave. Stories help to shed light on the world so that we can make sense of it. Have your parents ever told you about your family's **history**? Did your mother and father tell you how they first met or about the day you were born? Did they tell you what you were like as a baby? Without stories, we wouldn't know who we are.

---

1. All of the bolded words in this book (other than category titles) are in the glossary at the back of the book.

Do you know how the earth appeared in space? Was it always there, the third planet from the sun, making its way around the Milky Way galaxy? Or was there a time when the universe "gave birth" to our planet? What about the earliest human civilizations? Did people always drive cars and fly in airplanes? Was there a time when windows didn't even have glass? Do you know how the United States got its start? Did America always have fifty states?

If you know the answers to these questions, it's because you have been told narratives. Nothing would make sense without them. When we dream at night, we dream in stories. When we remember a happy memory, we remember in stories. When we learn our lessons, we learn in stories. When we tattle on a classmate, we tell the story of his rude behavior. Our very lives are stories in the making.

In this world, there are all kinds of stories. We've already taken a careful look at **fables** in *Writing & Rhetoric: Fable*.

▶ Do you remember the definition of a "fable"?

Even though fables are certainly fabulous, we would be sorry if they were the only type of story in this world. What would we do without detectives and cowgirls, princesses and pirates, superheroes and knights? Happily, the world is full of all kinds of stories. The more you listen to these stories, the bigger your imagination will grow. The bigger your imagination, the better you can tell your own stories. Who knows? Someday you might become a master storyteller yourself.

▶ Can you think of some other types of stories?

If you love adventure, you can hardly do better than a **fairy tale**. These stories were created especially for children, and they are full of magical people (such as fairy godmothers) and magical creatures (such as unicorns). Most fairy tales reward the good characters with splendid weddings or fabulous riches so that they live "happily ever after." The bad characters usually suffer terrible, but well-deserved, endings. In the original *Cinderella*, for example, the cinder girl marries the handsome prince, and the wicked stepsisters have their eyes pecked out by pigeons.

Myths are another important type of story. When you read about gods, goddesses, and **mortal** heroes, you probably have a book of mythology in your hands. Myths were used by ancient people to explain the beginning of things that could not easily be explained. Why are there seasons? Where did people come from? How did the mountains form? What causes lightning and thunder? Storytellers, such as the blind poet Homer, also created myths to give a glorious past to their ancestors. Myths are almost never about actual events, but the people who created them often believed them with religious faith.

Strange as it may seem, history is a type of story as well. The word "story" even has its roots in the word "history." With history, the storyteller is trying to tell about events that really happened or a person that really lived. The ancient Greeks wrote histories about their civilization. Herodotus, in particular, is known as the Father of History. He is one of the first writers to record the causes and events of a real war—the clash between Persia and Greece.

Parables are another form of story that you most likely know about. We will discuss parables in our next lesson.

The main thing that all stories have in common is a <u>beginning</u>, a <u>middle</u>, and an <u>end</u>. In other words, the events of a story usually happen in order according to some sort of plan.

If a day were a story, the sunrise would be the beginning. Noon would be the middle.

▶ And what would be the end?

One of the most famous story beginnings is found in Homer's long poem, *The Odyssey*.

> Tell me, O Muse, of that ingenious hero who travelled far and
> wide after he had sacked the famous town of Troy. Many cities
> did he visit, and many were the nations . . .

Of course, *The Odyssey* wouldn't be much of a story if the hero, Odysseus, simply climbed on board his ship and sailed straight home. Along the way, he meets all sorts of trouble: a one-eyed giant, a six-headed sea monster, a terrible sucking whirlpool, huge storms, and scary witches. These troubles form the middle of the story. And what about the ending? Well, the ending is equally famous. Odysseus returns home, only to find his palace filled with bad men. He must fight the bad men and drive them from his home before he can, at last, embrace his wife and enjoy peace and quiet.

Beginning. Middle. End. In this book, you'll have a chance to work on each part. So now let's get to it!

Tell It Back—Narration

Without looking at the text, tell what you know about these five words:
- Narrative
- Fable
- Fairy tale
- History
- Myth

Talk About It—

To answer the following questions, please refer to these story types:
- Narrative—All forms of story, from fairy tale, to history, to myths, to parables, to fables.
- Fable—A short story that teaches a simple moral lesson, usually with talking animals.
- Fairy tale—A fanciful story for children, usually with magical people or creatures.
- History—A narrative of actual events.
- Myth—An ancient story not based on actual events, with gods, goddesses, and heroes.

1. What type of story would be best if you wanted to tell about the San Francisco Earthquake of 1906? Why?

2. What type of story would be best if you wanted to warn children not to talk to strangers? Why?

3. What type of story would you most likely find on stone tablets found in a temple in ancient Egypt. Why?

Lesson 1: All Kinds of Stories

4. In what type of story would you encounter fire-breathing dragons, dwarves, and magic mirrors?

5. What type of story do you like best? Why?

Go Deeper—

1. Each of these narratives represents a certain type of story. Label the following paragraphs as fable, fairy tale, history, or myth.

_____ An eagle was shot in the breast by an arrow. As he lay dying, he turned his eyes to the arrow and saw his own feather on the shaft. "Ah!" he cried. "How cruel that I should be the cause of my own death!"

_____ In the middle of summer, a terrible disease began to show itself in the city of Athens. People in good health were all of a sudden attacked by violent fevers, and redness and swelling in the eyes.

_____ The fisherman shook the jar to find out what was inside. Presently smoke poured out and spiraled toward heaven. When the smoke reached its full height, the thick vapor condensed and became a huge genie. His head was like a dome, his hands like pitchforks, his legs as long as masts, and his mouth as big as a cave.

_____ The god Dionysus wanted to reward King Midas for his hospitality. So he said, "Ask for one wish and I will grant it." The greedy king replied, "Oh, honored god, I would be happy forever if everything I touched turned to gold."

_____ Athena was the goddess of wisdom, but on one occasion she did a very foolish thing. She entered into a competition with the goddesses Hera and Aphrodite for the prize of beauty.

_____ Jack jumped down and got hold of the ax and gave a chop at the beanstalk which cut it halfway through. The ogre felt the beanstalk shake and quiver so he stopped to see what was the matter. Then Jack gave another chop with the ax, and the beanstalk was cut in two and began to topple over. Then the ogre fell down and broke his crown, and the beanstalk came toppling after.

_____ On August 17, 1807, a curious crowd of people in New York gathered at a boat landing. Tied to the dock was a strange-looking craft. A smokestack rose above the deck. From the sides of the boat, there stood out queer-shaped paddle wheels. Of a sudden, the clouds of smoke from the smokestack grew larger, the paddle wheels turned, and the boat, to the astonishment of all, moved.

_____ A wolf one day saw his shadow, which was made large by the setting sun. "See how big I am!" he exclaimed. "Fancy me running away from a puny lion! I'll show him who is fit to be king of the beasts." Just then a huge shadow blotted him out entirely and the next instant a lion struck him down with a single blow.

_____ Mounted on a fine warhorse and clad in white armor from head to foot, Joan rode along past the cheering crowds. In one hand she carried an ancient sword that she had found near the tomb of a saint, and in the other a white banner sewn with lilies. The rough soldiers who were near her stopped swearing and treated her with their very best manners.

2. If you can clearly see the plan (or outline) of a story, you will become a better story planner yourself. Based on the clues in the following passages, try to identify the beginning, the middle, and the end of each story. It will help if you are familiar with the stories. Use *B* for beginning, *M* for middle, and *E* for end. Hint: All of these stories have happy endings. The middles of these stories always carry on what got started in the beginning.

Lesson 1: All Kinds of Stories

The Tortoise and the Hare —A fable from *Aesop's Fables*

_____ A hare was making fun of a tortoise one day for being so slow. But the tortoise said, "I get where I'm going sooner than you think. I'll run a race with you to prove it." The hare was much amused at the idea of running a race with the tortoise, but for the fun of the thing he agreed.

_____ The hare was soon out of sight, running as fast as the wind. Seeing the tortoise nowhere in sight, the hare lay down beside the road to take a nap and give the tortoise a chance to catch up. Meanwhile, the tortoise kept jogging slowly but steadily.

_____ When the hare woke up at last, he saw the tortoise nearing the finish line. The hare now ran his swiftest, but he could not catch up with the tortoise in time.

Cinderella —A fairy tale from The Brothers Grimm

_____ Then Cinderella seated herself on a stool and put her foot into the slipper, which fitted like a glove. When she rose up, the prince looked at her face and recognized her as the beautiful maiden he had danced with. The prince cried, "She will be my bride!"

_____ When Cinderella came to live with her stepsisters, she had to do hard work from morning till night. She had to get up before daybreak, carry water, light fires, cook, and wash. Besides this, the stepsisters mocked her and emptied her peas into the ashes, so that she was forced to sit and pick them out again. In the evening, when Cinderella had worked till she was weary, she had no bed to go to, but had to sleep by the hearth in the cinders.

_____ At the ball, the prince approached Cinderella and, with a bow, said, "Would you dance with me?" Then he took her by the hand and they twirled across the floor. The prince would dance with no other maiden, and never let loose of her hand.

Black Beauty —Adapted from a novel (with the same name) by Anna Sewell about a horse

_____ I was sold to a corn dealer and baker . . . One day I was loaded more than usual, and part of the road was a steep uphill. I used all my strength, but I could not get on, and was obliged continually to stop. This did not please my driver, and he laid his whip on badly. "Get on, you lazy fellow," he said, "or I'll make you." Again I started the heavy load, and struggled on a few yards; again the whip came down, and again I struggled forward. The pain of that great cart whip was sharp, but my mind was hurt quite as much as my poor sides.

_____ My troubles are all over, and I am at home; and often before I am quite awake, I fancy I am still in the orchard at my childhood home, standing with my old friends under the apple trees.

_____ While I was young I lived upon my mother's milk, as I could not eat grass. In the daytime I ran by her side, and at night I lay down close by her. When it was hot we used to stand by the pond in the shade of the trees, and when it was cold we had a nice warm shed near the grove.

The Myth of the Minotaur —A myth from Ancient Greece

_____ In the darkness, Theseus heard the Minotaur breathing. He waited against the wall and saw two eyes, glowing red like flames, moving slowly toward him. With a sudden leap, Theseus struck with his sword. The Minotaur fell dead to the ground. Safe at last, the Hero started on his way back to daylight.

_____ In the polis of Athens, there lived a young prince by the name of Theseus. As the son of the king of Athens, Theseus could have lived a soft and easy life, but instead he dreamed of brave deeds and daring adventures. His first test was not long in coming. Athens had a problem. On the island of Crete, a labyrinth had been constructed to contain the terrible Minotaur. The Minotaur was a monster with a man's body and a bull's head, and it fed on human flesh.

Lesson 1: All Kinds of Stories

Every year, the Athenians were forced to send seven youths and seven maids to Crete, where they would be eaten by the Minotaur in his labyrinth.

_____ Theseus vowed that he would slay the Minotaur himself or die trying. The maiden Ariadne gave the hero a sword and a ball of thread. "Use the thread to find your way out of the labyrinth again," she said. "Its halls are long and dark and it is easy to get lost. Beware of the Minotaur, for he can smell human flesh."

Speak It—

Memorize the definition of the following narrative forms and say them aloud to your teacher or to a classmate. Or you can practice the definitions by recording them with your favorite audio device, and playing them back.

Narrative—All forms of story, from fairy tale, to history, to myths, to parables, to fables.

Fable—A short story that teaches a simple moral lesson, usually with talking animals.

Fairy tale—A fanciful story for children, usually with magical people or creatures.

History—A narrative of actual events.

Myth—An ancient story not based on actual events, with gods, goddesses, and heroes.

Lesson 2

A Long Parable

Along with fables, myths, fairy tales, and histories, another important form of narrative is the parable. If you have ever read or heard stories from the Christian Scriptures, you know that many of these famous stories are parables.

▶ You might even know who was famous for telling parables. Can you guess?

If you answered, "Jesus" (born sometime between 3 and 6 BC), you are correct.

Parables are similar to fables—they are also short stories meant to teach moral lessons—but unlike fables they are always true to life. Parables never include talking lambs or racing tortoises as fables do. Nor do they include flying carpets, magic beans, or wicked dwarves as fairy tales do. Nor do parables include gods of the sea or gods of the air or monsters with snakes for hair as myths do. Instead, parables tell stories that could have happened in real life and that teach a moral lesson.

Jesus spoke in parables to make big ideas understandable to ordinary people. But not everybody understood Jesus's parables. His enemies were often confused by them. Like a sword with two edges, parables had a way of making things clear to Jesus's friends and frustrating to the minds of His enemies.

10

You will not find any simple morals or proverbs after a parable. Unlike fables, the morals of parables are not easy to explain with a proverb. Most parables illustrate the love of God and the idea of the kingdom of heaven, which Jesus said was coming.

Fable	Parable
Talking animals—represent human vice or virtue	True to life—set in the real world
How to be wise—Simple moral or ethical lesson	Complex moral or spiritual lesson, basic truth

What are some of Jesus's most famous parables? *The Good Samaritan. The Lost Sheep. The Sower.* In this lesson, we'll take a close look at *The Prodigal Son.*

The Prodigal Son

—Retold by George Hodges, adapted from his *When the King Came: Stories from the Four Gospels*, 1904; Luke 15:11-32

Once upon a time, there was a man who had two sons. The elder son was quiet and steady, but the younger son was a restless lad who was weary of staying at home, and wished to go and see the world. So the younger son went one day to his father and asked for the money that would properly come to him when he was older. "Father," he said, "give me my share of your estate." And the father, who was a man of wealth, gave the younger son what he had been saving for him.

Then the younger son took his money, and he went a long way off into the great world, where he had a fine time. He spent his money on rich clothing and expensive lodgings, buying whatever was sweet to eat and sour to drink. All he thought about was how to have an even better time the next day. And so the days went by. Some of the sweets gave him a toothache, and some of the sours gave him a headache, and none of the pleasures lasted long; but he fancied that he was enjoying them all. At

Lesson 2: A Long Parable

last, one morning, he woke up to find that he had not a penny in his pocket. All the money his father had given him was gone.

And then something dreadful happened. In that land, there arose a mighty famine. Now a famine, as you probably know, is a time when everybody is hungry and there is nothing to eat. There had been no rain. The grain had stopped growing, and the grass had stopped growing, and everything had ceased to grow, except people's appetites—they grew bigger and bigger.

This was very hard for the lad who had spent all his money. Moreover, he found that in losing his wealth he had lost his friends also. All the fun-loving young men and women to whom he had given so many gifts now turned their backs upon him. When they saw him in the street, they went around the corner to avoid him. After all, they had been only friends of his money. Indeed, the younger son himself had not been a true friend to them either. He had never really cared about anybody but himself. He had never helped another; so now there was none who would help him.

Only one course was open to the younger son if he didn't want to starve—he had to go to work. But even work was hard to find. He did not know enough to do skilled work, such as pottery or carpentry. In spite of his fine clothes and his soft hands, he could do nothing but unskilled work. That is the hardest kind of work and the worst paid. In the end, the only job he could find was that of a swineherd. Day after day, in sun and rain, he tended pigs in the field. And because it was a time of famine, when food was failing even in rich houses, he had to have his dinner with the pigs. Now a menu for a pig's dinner is not a pleasant meal for a man, even when the trough is full to the brim. Think, then, what it must have been like in the middle of a famine. The swine had husks, and the **prodigal** son had nothing better to eat. The farmer came out with a bucketful of husks and dumped them down upon the ground, and the boy and the pigs fought together for the best pieces.

Then the prodigal son thought of home. He could shut his eyes and see how it all looked: the house where he was born, with trees about it; the rooms within, and all the familiar furniture; the table spread for dinner, and his father and mother and elder brother sitting down. Was there a place left for him? Why, even his father's servants had enough food to spare, and here he was, perishing with hunger.

Finally, he could stand it no longer. The prodigal son said to himself, "I will go home. I will go to my father, and will say to him, 'Father, I have sinned against heaven and before you, and am no longer worthy to be called thy son. Make me as one of thy hired servants.'" So he filled his pockets with husks, and shut the gate upon the swine, and turned his face toward home.

Now that day his father was looking and looking down the road. It had been many months since he had heard from the younger son, and the last news had not been pleasant news. So he watched the road, saying to himself, "Someday he will come back." Away down the street, walking slowly, like one who is weary after a long journey, or like one who is very doubtful if he will be welcome, came a man: probably a tramp, for his clothes were ragged and dirty, and yet with a familiar look. And the father looked again, and behold, it was his younger son.

What did the father do? Did he say, "There is my bad son! There is the son who has disgraced himself and me! He has spent all his money and is coming back for more. He  thinks that I will forgive him, but he will find that he is very much mistaken." No! He jumped up instantly, running out of the house and down the road, so that he met his prodigal son while the lad was yet a great way from the house. He had compassion, and greeted him, and put his arms around him and kissed him. And the prodigal son began to say the words which he had been repeating to himself, "Father, I have sinned against heaven and in your sight, and am no more worthy to be called your son." But the father brought him in, and called the servants. "Bring forth the best robe," he said, "and put it on him; and put a ring on his hand and shoes on his feet; and bring here the fatted calf, and kill it, and let us eat, and be merry."

So the servants cooked the very nicest dinner which they knew how to make, and the neighbors were sent for; and after dinner men were brought in with banjos and violins, and all began to dance.

There was one exception, however, to this merriment. That was the elder son. He was working in the field, knowing nothing of this great event. When he came home to supper, the elder son was much surprised to hear a great noise of talking and laughing, with music and dancing. All the young men and women of the neighborhood seemed to

Lesson 2: A Long Parable

be there, having a beautiful time. The elder son thought it strange that there should be a party at his house, and he not be invited. So he called one of the servants and asked what these things meant. And the servant said, "Your brother is come; and your father has killed the fatted calf, because he has received him safe and sound."

But the elder son was angry, and would not go in. "My brother has been a fool," he said to himself, "and bad besides. Now he comes home and my father takes him in and makes much of him. My brother ought to have a whipping instead of a supper."

Then the father left the guests and the dancing, and came out and spoke to his angry elder son. And the elder son said to his father, "All these years I've stayed quietly at home, and minded your business, working early and late upon the farm, and never disobeying you. And you have never given any party for me. You have never made a supper that I might be merry with my friends. And now your worthless son has come, who has wasted your money in fooling around and getting drunk, and you are giving him the best you have."

But the Father said, "Son, you are always with me, and all that I have is yours. It was fitting that we should make merry and be glad; for your brother was dead and is alive again; and was lost, and is found."

Tell It Back—Narration

1. Without looking at the parable, tell back *The Prodigal Son* as best as you can remember it using your own words and any words from the story. For further practice, you could record your "telling it back" and play it afterwards.
   - Keep the events of the story in their proper order.

Here are the first two sentences to get you started:

Once upon a time, there was a man who had two sons. The elder son was quiet and steady, but the younger son was a restless lad who was weary of staying at home, and wished to go and see the world.

2. Put the events in order below, using *B* for beginning, *M* for middle, and *E* for end.

_____ Only one course was open to the boy, except to starve, and that was to go to work. In the end, the only job he could find was that of a swineherd.

_____ The father said, "Son, you are always with me, and all that I have is yours. It was fitting that we should make merry and be glad; for your brother was dead and is alive again; and was lost, and is found."

_____ Once upon a time, there was a man who had two sons. The elder son was quiet and steady, but the younger son was a restless lad who was weary of staying at home, and wished to go and see the world.

3. **WRITTEN NARRATIVE**

   a. Write your own sentence to tell what happens at the <u>beginning</u> of the story.

   _____

   _____

   _____

   b. Write your own sentence to tell what happens in the <u>middle</u> of the story.

   _____

   _____

   _____

   c. Write your own sentence to tell what happens at the <u>end</u> of the story.

   _____

   _____

   _____

Lesson 2: A Long Parable

Talk About It—

1. How would you spend your money if you were suddenly given a large fortune?

2. What do you think happens in the end of this story? Is the older brother persuaded to join the feast, or does he remain in the courtyard, angry and unforgiving?

3. Examine the painting *The Return of the Prodigal Son* by Rembrandt van Rijn, painted around 1667. Why do you suppose the boy's hair has been shaved off? Why is one of his sandals on and the other one off? Why do you suppose he's not looking up into his father's face? Who is the man standing on the right?

Go Deeper—

1. The word "prodigal" comes from the Latin word *prodigus*, which is a combined word meaning "to drive away" or "scatter." Because the prodigal son scatters his money and his life on foolish things, the word "prodigal" probably means:
   a. sensible
   b. friendly
   c. wasteful
   d. heroic

2. Use the word "prodigal" in your own complete sentence. Be sure that the meaning of the word is clear.

   _____

   _____

3. The father in this story could have sent his younger son away or made him work like a servant. Instead, he had compassion and welcomed him home with open arms. Which words mean nearly the same thing as compassion?

    a. anger and punishment

    b. care and kindness

    c. sorrow and sadness

    d. laughter and happiness

4. Circle the adjectives that best describe the younger son at the beginning of the parable.

    selfish and careless   kind and generous

    bold and brave   dirty and smelly

5. Circle the adjectives that best describe the younger son as he returns home in the middle of the parable.

    scared and cowardly   ashamed and sorry

    happy and excited   goofy and silly

6. How do you think the younger son felt at the end of the parable?

    a. greedy for more money

    b. ready for more fun and parties

    c. frightened that his father would make him a servant

    d. safe in his father's love

7. Do you think the younger son will change his ways or will he remain the same? Explain your answer using complete sentences.

    change his ways   remain the same

    _____

    _____

    _____

    _____

8. Does the father change during the story or does he always stay the same? Explain your answer using complete sentences.

he changes   he always stays the same

_____

_____

_____

_____

9. The father in this story stands for someone. The father is like:
   a. an angry old man
   b. a greedy king
   c. a loving God
   d. a kind soldier

10. The characters in *The Prodigal Son* are imaginary or make-believe people. They never really existed. The word **fiction** is often used to describe an imaginary story. And yet, even though the story is fiction, Jesus uses it to illustrate something He believes is true. What do you suppose is true of the story?
    a. The father hates the prodigal son and wants to destroy him.
    b. The father loves the prodigal son and rejoices when he comes back home.
    c. The father wants the prodigal son to earn his love by working hard like a servant.
    d. The father wants the prodigal son to stay far away and never come home.

11. Which two of these verses from the Hebrew Scriptures do you think best expresses the main idea of *The Prodigal Son*?
    a. "Go and cry out to the [false] gods you have chosen. Let them save you when you are in trouble!"—Judges 10:14
    b. "The LORD your God is with you,/ he is mighty to save./ He will take great delight in you,/ he will quiet you with his love,/ he will rejoice over you with singing."—Zephaniah 3:17

c. "He who loves pleasure will become poor."—Proverbs 21:17

d. "Some trust in chariots and some in horses,/ but we trust in the name of the LORD our God."—Psalm 20:7

Writing Time—

1. **COPYWORK**—Neatly copy the sentence in the space provided:

Some of the sweets gave him a toothache, and some of the sours gave him a headache, and none of the pleasures lasted long.

_____

_____

_____

_____

_____

2. **DICTATION**—Your teacher will read a little part of *The Prodigal Son* back to you. Please listen carefully! After your teacher reads once, she will read slowly again and include the punctuation marks. Your task will be to write down the sentences as your teacher reads them one by one.

_____

_____

_____

_____

_____

3. **SENTENCE PLAY**—<u>Then the prodigal son thought of home. He could shut his eyes and see how it all looked: the house where he was born, the rooms within, and the table spread for dinner.</u>

a. What if, instead of home, the prodigal son thought about an amusement park? What three things would he see when he closed his eyes?

Using the three things that you just came up with, write a complete sentence describing what the prodigal son might have seen.

Then the prodigal son thought of an amusement park. He could shut his eyes and see how it all looked:

_____

_____

_____

_____

b. What would the prodigal son see if he thought of a modern city? In a complete sentence, describe what he would see.

Then the prodigal son thought of a modern city. He could shut his eyes and see how it all looked:

_____

_____

_____

_____

c. What would the prodigal son see if he thought of a farm? In a complete sentence, describe what he would see.

Then the prodigal son thought of a farm. He could close his eyes and remember the whole thing:

_____

_____

_____

_____

_____

4. **COPIOUSNESS**—Do you remember the meaning of the word "copiousness"? It means "plenty" or "lots of something." Again, these exercises are designed to help you reach for new words to express the same ideas. The more ways in which you can say something, the more lively and exciting your writing will be. Who would be happy with "The weather is good," when one could say, "What a gloriously beautiful day!" Would you say to the hairdresser, "I'd like a nice haircut, please," when you could be precise and say, "I'd like a super short hairdo and please dye it hot pink." To say, "I'm bleeding," is not nearly as helpful as to say, "I've got blood spurting from my left upper arm." Copiousness is important, not only in writing interestingly, but also in learning to say exactly what you mean.

In our first efforts, just as before, we are going to work on exchanging our nouns and adjectives with **synonyms**. A synonym is a word that has nearly the same meaning as another word. So, a "kid" is a "youngster" is a "child"— these are all synonyms.

You can swap these words around. Did the <u>kid</u> like the pickles? Did the <u>youngster</u> like the pickles? Does the <u>child</u> like the pickles? One word may be better than another, depending on the situation, but folks are still going to get the picture. A "brat" is not a synonym for <u>child</u> unless you want to say that all the children in a particular story are brats. This is because a brat is a "naughty child" whereas a child is just a child. He could be well-behaved or naughty.

▶ What are synonyms for the nouns "father" and "mother"? What is a synonym for the adjective "funny"?

Do you remember our definitions? A noun is a person, place, thing, or idea. An adjective adds description to a noun and helps us to "see" it more clearly. If you have "true love," "love" is the noun because it is an idea and "true" is an adjective because it describes what kind of love it is.

When in doubt about whether a word might be a noun or an adjective, take a familiar noun, such as "cookie," and place a word in front of it. If the word describes the cookie, then it is an adjective: "new" cookie, "purple" cookie, "big" cookie, "man-eating" cookie, "raisin" cookie.

▶ <u>Circle</u> the nouns and <u>underline</u> the adjectives:

taffy	desk	snake	dangerous	strange	girl
delicious	book	bright	cheerful	sticky	mountain
rude	pastor	baby	sweet	kindness	city
silly	soup	pencil	night	rainbow	chilly

5. Mark the nouns and adjective in the sentence below. Place an *N* over the nouns and an *ADJ* over the adjective.

In that land, there arose a mighty famine.

6. Next, replace the adjective "mighty" with different adjectives that have close to the same meaning. Replace any nouns below that are left blank with different nouns that make sense.

a. In that land, there arose a(n) _____ famine.
   (adjective for mighty)

b. In that land, there arose a(n) _____ famine.
   (adjective for mighty)

c. In that _____, there arose a(n)
   (noun for land)

   _____ famine.
   (adjective for mighty)

7. Mark the nouns in the following sentence with an *N*. Then, write the sentence three times, adding a different adjective in front of each of the three nouns every time:

The son tended pigs in the field.

Example: The tiny son tended giant pigs in the muddy field.

a. _____

   _____.

b. _____

   _____.

c. _____

   _____.

8. Rewrite the sentence with different subjects. A subject tells what the sentence is about.

Example: The sheep were chased by the daughter in the pen.

Rewrite #1: The daughter chased the sheep in the pen.

Rewrite #2: The pen held the sheep as they were chased by the daughter.

Now it's your turn. Rewrite the following sentence using the subjects indicated ("the son" and "the field"):

The pigs were tended by the son in the field.

a. The son _____.

b. The field _____

_____.

9. **POINT OF VIEW**—The prodigal son is told in the <u>third-person point of view</u>: "he," "she," "it," "they." Tell the ending of the parable in <u>first-person view</u> ("I," "we") as if you, the storyteller, are the older brother.

When the older brother came near the house, he heard music and dancing and happy voices. He called one of the servants and asked him what was going on. "Your younger brother has come home," he replied, "and your father has killed a fat calf for a party because he is back home safe and sound."

The older brother became angry and refused to go in. So his father went out and pleaded with him. But he answered his father, "Look! All these years I've been slaving for you and never disobeyed your orders. Yet you never killed even a young goat so I could celebrate with my friends. But when this son of yours who has thrown away your money with wicked people comes home, you kill a fat calf for him!"

"My son," the father said, "you are always with me, and everything I have is yours. But we have to celebrate and be glad, because this brother of yours was dead and is alive again; he was lost and is found."

_____

_____

_____

Speak It—

Read your retelling of *The Prodigal Son*'s ending to your class, teacher, or recording device. Discuss how first-person point of view changes the parable.

Lesson 3 ·

A Short Parable

In *Writing & Rhetoric: Fable*, we learned that foolish creatures can take many forms. There are stubborn fools such as the ass, quarrelsome fools such as the young bulls, greedy fools such as the dog, and trickster fools such as the shepherd boy. In this lesson, we meet a foolish man who is similar to the greedy dog.

The Rich Fool is another well-known parable from the Christian New Testament. Whereas *The Prodigal Son* and *The Good Samaritan* are two of Jesus's longest parables, *The Rich Fool* is very short. And yet *The Rich Fool* is quite a powerful story for its size.

The Rich Fool

(Luke 12:16-21)

The ground of a certain rich man produced a good crop. He thought to himself, "What shall I do? I have no place to store my crops." Then he said, "This is what I'll do. I will tear down my barns and build bigger ones, and there I will store all my grain and my goods. And I'll say to myself, 'You have plenty of good things laid up for many years. Take life easy; eat, drink, and be merry.'"

But God said to him, "You fool! This very night your life will be demanded from you. Then who will get what you have prepared for yourself?"

This is how it will be with anyone who stores up things for himself but is not rich toward God.

Tell It Back—Narration

1. **ORAL NARRATION**—Without looking at the parable, tell back *The Rich Fool* as best as you can remember it using your own words and any words from the

story. For additional practice, record your telling back on your favorite device and play it afterwards.

- Keep the events of the story in their proper order.

Here is the first sentence to get you started:

The ground of a certain rich man produced a good crop.

2. **WRITTEN NARRATION**

a. Write your own sentence to tell what happens at the <u>beginning</u> of the story.

_____

_____

_____

b. Write your own sentence to tell what happens in the <u>middle</u> of the story.

_____

_____

_____

c. Write your own sentence to tell what happens at the <u>end</u> of the story.

_____

_____

_____

Talk About It—

1. Do you remember the fable of *The Dog and Her Reflection*? While crossing a bridge with a bone in her mouth, the greedy Dog saw her reflection in the river. And then what happened? The Dog dropped the real bone as she tried to steal

the bone from her reflection. In what ways is the parable of *The Rich Fool* similar to the fable of *The Dog and Her Reflection*? In what ways is it different?

2. Why do you think God is angry with the rich man for storing up things for himself? What do you think he could have done with his crop instead of tearing down his old barns and building bigger ones?

3. Both the father in *The Prodigal Son* and the rich man in *The Rich Fool* are very wealthy men. And yet the father is a good character and the rich man is a foolish character. How are the two rich men different so that one is praiseworthy and the other is blameworthy?

4. An American named Howard Hughes became one of the first billionaires in history. In other words, he had over a billion dollars or $1,000,000,000 to his name. He owned hotels, movie studios, factories, and airline companies. He should have been fabulously happy, right? Well, Howard Hughes may have been one of the richest men on the planet, but he spent his last years lonely and sad. Like the prodigal son, he couldn't trust any of his so-called friends. Perhaps they only loved him for his money. Would you rather be very rich (like Howard Hughes), very poor, or somewhere in the middle? Why?

Go Deeper—

1. What does this sentence mean? "This very night your life will be demanded from you."

   It means, "This very night _____."

2. What is the main idea of this story?
   a. Store up as much money as you can, for life is short.
   b. Spend money only on yourself.
   c. Never ever enjoy your money or your blessings.
   d. Be generous with the gifts you have been given.

3. Which of these famous sayings do you think best expresses the main idea of *The Rich Fool*?

    a. "Whoever trusts in riches will fall."

    b. "Praise is not a pudding you can eat."

    c. "Never encourage a fool to do wrong."

    d. "The apple doesn't fall far from the tree."

4. The rich man is called a <u>fool</u>. Write your own definition of a "fool."

    Fool (fül) n. ▶ _____

    _____

5. Now look up the word "fool" in a dictionary and write it down. Is your definition similar to the dictionary definition?

    Fool (fül) n. ▶ _____

    _____

Writing Time—

1. **COPYWORK**—Neatly copy the sentences in the space provided:

I'll say to myself, "You have plenty of good things laid up for many years. Take life easy; eat, drink, and be merry."

_____

_____

_____

_____

_____

_____

_____

2. **DICTATION**—Your teacher will read a little part of *The Rich Fool* back to you. Please listen carefully! After your teacher reads once, she will read slowly again and include the punctuation marks. Your task will be to write down the sentences as your teacher reads them one by one.

_____

_____

_____

_____

_____

_____

_____

_____

3. **SENTENCE PLAY**

In *The Prodigal Son*, we saw how a foolish young man spends his money. In *The Rich Fool*, we see how a foolish rich man gives himself bad advice:

"Take life easy; eat, drink, and be merry."

Using the sentence above as a model, fill in new commands for a modern rich man to be giving to himself. What else could he say to show his foolishness? For example, the sentence could read, "Go rest by a swimming pool; sleep, swim, and sleep some more."

_____

_____

_____

4. COPIOUSNESS

We learned about synonyms in our last lesson. For example, we know that a synonym for the noun "lollipop" is "sucker." We know that a synonym for the adjective "creepy" is "weird."

As best as you can remember, write the definition of a synonym, a noun, and an adjective in the spaces below. Use complete sentences.

SYNONYM

_____

NOUN

_____

ADJECTIVE

_____

5. Just as nouns and adjectives do, verbs can also have synonyms. A verb is often the action word of the sentence: *run, slide, kick, dance, fly, fall, bump, laugh, cry.* The word "jump" is a verb. Synonyms for jump include "leap," "hop," "skip," and "bound." Underline the verbs, the action words, in each sentence below. These sentences are adapted from Proverbs 14 of the Hebrew Scriptures.

    a. The wise woman builds her house.

    b. With her own hands, the foolish woman tears her house down.

    c. A truthful witness speaks honestly.

    d. A false witness pours out lies.

    e. A wise man shuns evil.

    f. A fool's talk brings a rod to his back.

    g. The lips of the wise protect them.

Lesson 3: A Short Parable

6. Mark the nouns (2), adjective (1), and verbs (2) in the sentence below. Place an *N* over the nouns, *ADJ* over the adjective, and *V* over the verbs.

I will tear down my barns and build bigger ones.

a. Use synonyms to replace the words you marked and rewrite the sentence. Remember that a synonym is a word that has nearly the same meaning as another word.

_____

_____

_____

b. Use a thesaurus to help yourself write another variation of the same sentence.

_____

_____

_____

c. Using "I" as the subject, rewrite the following sentences but keep the same meaning. A <u>subject</u> tells what the sentence is about.

Example: My geese will be fed by me.
Changes to: I will feed my geese.

My barns will be torn down by me.

I _____

_____

My barns will be built into bigger ones by me.

I _____

_____

7. **AMPLIFICATION**—In many ways, *The Rich Fool* is like the summary of a much longer story—a story that could go on for pages and pages. Don't you want to know why the rich man is so greedy? Don't you want to know if he had a wife and kids? Does he live like a king or does he live like a miser, saving every little penny? Details such as these make a story come to life.

Take this parable and write it with more details. What sort of crop does the rich man harvest? How many acres of land does he own? How many servants and laborers work for him? How big are his barns and how much bigger does he want to build them? How does the rich man react when he is called a fool by God? Where is he? In bed? At his dining room table? By his swimming pool?

The Rich Fool

The ground of a certain rich man produced a good crop. He thought to himself, "What shall I do? I have no place to store my crops." Then he said, "This is what I'll do. I will tear down my barns and build bigger ones, and there I will store all my grain and my goods. And I'll say to myself, 'You have plenty of good things laid up for many years. Take life easy; eat, drink, and be merry.'"

But God said to him, "You fool! This very night your life will be demanded from you. Then who will get what you have prepared for yourself?"

This is how it will be with anyone who stores up things for himself but is not rich toward God.

_____

_____

_____

_____

8. Read *The Rich Fool* again. Imagine if the rich man had been a wise man instead of a fool. How would he have spent his money differently? Now write a short story with the same beginning, but a different middle and a different end.

The Rich Sage

Sage = A wise person

The ground of a certain rich man produced a good crop. He thought to himself, "What shall I do? I have no place to store my crops."

_____

_____

_____

_____

_____

_____

_____

_____

_____

_____

_____

_____

_____

_____

_____

_____

_____

_____

_____

_____

_____

_____

_____

_____

_____

_____

_____

_____

_____

_____

_____

Speak It—

REVERSE NARRATION

Your teacher will read *The Rich Fool* again. Listen carefully to the order of events: <u>beginning</u>, <u>middle</u>, and <u>end</u>. Now let's try something a little strange. Narrate the parable of *The Rich Fool* back to a partner, a recording device, or to your class going in this order: end, middle, and beginning. Can you do it?

Lesson 4 ···

Main Idea—Parables

More often than not, writers write and speakers speak because they want to say something important to you. They want you, the reader or listener, to learn something or believe something. Fable makers and parable makers both want to teach you "right from wrong," and "how to live your life." History writers want you to understand a message from times gone by. If a writer or speaker really doesn't have anything to say, she is called a blabbermouth or a gasbag or some other not-so-nice name.

The **main idea** is the most important thought a writer or speaker is trying to communicate. It is one of the ways in which we can summarize, or sum up, the lesson of a story.

Fables usually come with morals, which are their own ready-made main ideas. Parables contain main ideas, too, but—as we have said—they are more complex than a simple proverb. Still, we can be rewarded by trying to figure out the most important ideas in a parable. It's a little bit like solving a mystery. The parable contains a mystery and you have to figure out what it means.

The Lame Man and the Blind Man

Adapted from the Talmud

There once was a king who had an orchard of fine young fig trees. He appointed two gardeners to take care of the orchard—a lame man and a blind man. One day, while the king was away, the two gardeners hatched an idea. The lame man asked the blind man to put him on his shoulders and he would pluck the ripest fruit. So the lame man served as the blind man's eyes and the blind man served as the lame man's legs. Together they made a feast of the figs.

When the king returned, he immediately spotted the missing fruit. He demanded an explanation from his two gardeners. "I could not have taken the figs," said the lame man, "for I have no legs."

"I could not have taken the figs," said the blind man, "for I have no eyes."

What did the king, the lord of this garden, do? He had the lame man mount upon the back of the blind man and he judged them as one together. And they were both found guilty.

Tell It Back—**Narration**

Without looking at the parable, tell back *The Lame Man and the Blind Man* as best as you can remember it using your own words and any words from the story. For extra practice, you can also record it on your favorite device and play it back.

● Keep the events of the story in their proper order.

Here is the first sentence to get you started:

There once was a king who had an orchard of fine young fig trees.

Talk About It—

1. Why did the lame man and the blind man need each other?

2. Was one man more responsible for the crime of stealing figs, or were they equally responsible? Give a reason for your answer.

Go Deeper—

1. The following ideas are all true for this parable. What idea is the most important?

   a. Bad deeds will be found out.

   b. It is wrong to steal figs.

   c. Half a wrong is really a whole wrong.

   d. Never lie to someone who knows you're lying.

   ● Explain your answer to your teacher or your classmates.

2. Which proverb from the Talmud fits this parable as one possible moral?

   a. "Sin is sweet in the beginning, but bitter in the end."

   b. "Few people see their own faults."

   c. "Weak walls invite a thief."

   d. "If you tell a secret to three people, ten will know it."

3. Look carefully at this statue, *The Blindman and the Lame*, carved by Jean Turcan. Pretend for a moment that you don't know that these men are thieves. Does this statue have a main idea that might be different from the ideas above? Write a main idea in the space provided.

_____

_____

_____

_____

_____

_____

_____

_____

_____

The Crying Woman

A Chinese Parable

Once there was an old woman who cried all the time for her two daughters. Her oldest daughter was an umbrella maker and her youngest daughter was a noodle maker. When the days were sunny, she cried for her oldest daughter because no one would buy her umbrellas. When the days were rainy, she cried for her youngest daughter because it was impossible to dry noodles without the sun. The old woman cried so much that she became known to her neighbors as "the crying woman."

Lesson 4: *Main Idea—Parables*

One day she told her woes to a monk. "What am I to do?" she cried. "Rain or shine, I am never happy."

The kindly monk replied, "You must change the way you are looking at things. It is very simple. On rainy days, think of your oldest daughter who makes umbrellas and rejoice for her. She is selling many umbrellas. On sunny days, think of your youngest daughter who makes noodles and rejoice for her. She is drying many noodles in the sun."

The old woman took the monk's advice. She is now known as "the smiling woman." Rain or shine, she is always smiling.

Tell It Back—**Narration**

- Without looking at the parable, tell back *The Crying Woman* as best as you remember it using your own words and any words from the story. For extra practice, you can record your telling back into your favorite device and play it afterwards.
- Keep the events of the story in their proper order.

Here is the first sentence to get you started:

Once there was an old woman who cried all the time for her two daughters.

Talk About It—

1. Why is the crying woman always sad, rain or shine?
2. What is wrong with the way the crying woman looks at things?
3. How is this parable similar to *The Tale of the Chinese Farmer* from *Writing & Rhetoric: Fable*?
4. Have you ever thought that something was bad, but then it turned out to be good?

Go Deeper—

1. The following ideas are all true for *The Crying Woman*. What idea is the most important?

    a. It's best to look on the bright side of life.

    b. A woman who cries all the time will get a reputation for being sad.

    c. Good things can happen in rain or sunshine.

    d. People often make their own troubles.

    • Explain your answer to your teacher or classmates.

2. Which proverb from China fits this parable as one possible moral?

    a. "If no one plows, no one will harvest."

    b. "Nature can help you or harm you."

    c. "When a tree falls, the monkeys run away."

    d. "A bad worker blames his tools."

3. Look carefully at this painting *Great Bridge, Sudden Shower at Atake* by Japanese artist Utagawa Hiroshige. Does this painting have a main idea that might be different from the ideas above? Write a main idea in the space provided.

_____

_____

_____

_____

_____

_____

_____

Lesson 4: *Main Idea—Parables*

Lesson 5 ....

Dialogue— A Greek Myth

Some people talk a lot. Some talk only a little. And some people talk to themselves even when nobody else is around.

If you're like me, you enjoy listening in on other people's conversations. It's rather rude to do this in real life, but not at all if you happen to be reading a story. Readers often find **dialogue** to be the most interesting part of a book. It helps you to know what the characters are thinking and what they would sound like if you were there in the room with them.

Here's a nice tidbit of dialogue from *The Wonderful Wizard of Oz*:

> The little girl, seeing she had lost one of her pretty shoes, grew angry, and said to the witch, "Give me back my shoe!"
>
> "I will not," retorted the witch, "for it is now my shoe, and not yours."
>
> "You are a wicked creature!" cried Dorothy. "You have no right to take my shoe from me."

"I shall keep it, just the same," said the witch, laughing at her, "and someday I shall get the other one from you, too."

This made Dorothy so very angry that she picked up the bucket of water that stood near and dashed it over the witch, wetting her from head to foot.

Instantly the wicked woman gave a loud cry of fear, and then, as Dorothy looked at her in wonder, the witch began to shrink and fall away.

"See what you have done!" the witch screamed. "In a minute I shall melt away."

"I'm very sorry, indeed," said Dorothy, who was truly frightened to see the witch actually melting away like brown sugar before her very eyes.

You can see from the dialogue what a wicked creature the witch is. She steals a shoe and then teases Dorothy about it. And she must be terribly filthy and mean for a little water to melt her.

Dialogue is a conversation between two or more people. It is one of the best ways that a writer gives her writing more detail. **Monologue** is a long speech by one person, sometimes talking to himself, all alone.

It's easy to tell when characters are talking. The words in a dialogue are always surrounded by quotation marks like this: "abcdefg." They look like two little eyes, hanging in the air. Writers use quotation marks to let their readers know that their characters are talking to each other or talking to themselves.

Here is an example:

Mark Antony said, "This was the noblest Roman of them all."

Or the same statement can be written like this:

"This was the noblest Roman of all," Mark Antony said.

Now we are going to read a myth that lacks dialogue. While you read, see if you can find a good place to add some talking between the two characters.

Do you remember that ancient people told myths to explain the beginning of things? The great city of Athens began its history as a small fort on a hill known as the Acropolis. From the top of the Acropolis, it was easy to see the sea, the farms, and the fishing villages of Greece in every direction. In this myth, the Greeks, who worshipped Athena, try to explain how she came to be the protector goddess of Athens.

Do you remember the fable of *The Trees Choose a King* from the Hebrew Scriptures, which we covered in the last book—*Writing & Rhetoric: Fable*? The Olive Tree was one of the wise trees in that story. In this myth, the Greeks also try to explain the origin of the olive tree.

Athena Defeats Poseidon

Athena and Poseidon both knew that the small fortress town on top of the hill known as the Acropolis would someday be a famous city. Both gods wanted the honor of naming the town. Athena wanted it to be called Athens after herself. Poseidon, on the other hand, liked the sound of his own name much better.

The two gods quarreled and argued and quarreled some more. At last, they came up with a way to **resolve** their differences. They agreed to give gifts to the people of the town and allow them to decide which god would name the place.

So Poseidon created the horse and gave the people horses to help plow their fields and to carry men into battle. Athena created the olive tree.

Poseidon almost laughed to see a spindly tree contending against his magnificent new creature. And yet the Greeks found the fruit to be delicious—not only the fruit, but its oil as well. Olive oil could be used to fuel lamps, to make soap, to soothe sunburns, and to clean wounds. The wood of the tree could be carved into beautiful furniture.

In the end, the people voted for Athena's gift. To this day, the city surrounding the Acropolis is known as Athens.

Tell It Back—Narration

1. **ORAL NARRATION**—Without looking at the myth, tell back *Athena Defeats Poseidon* as best as you can remember it using your own words and any words from the story. For further practice, you can record it on your favorite device and play it back afterwards.

    • Keep the events of the story in their proper order.

   ## Here is the first sentence to get you started:

   Athena and Poseidon both knew that the small fortress town on top of the hill known as the Acropolis would someday be a famous city.

2. Put the events in order below using *B* for beginning, *M* for middle, and *E* for end.

   _____ In the end, the people voted for Athena's gift.

   _____ Both gods wanted the honor of naming the town.

   _____ Poseidon created the horse and gave the people horses to help plow their fields and to carry men into battle. Athena created the olive tree.

3. **WRITTEN NARRATION**

   a. Write your own sentence to tell what happens at the beginning of the story.

   _____

   _____

   _____

b. Write your own sentence to tell what happens in the middle of the story.

_____

_____

_____

c. Write your own sentence to tell what happens at the end of the story.

_____

_____

_____

Talk About It—

1. Can you tell the story of how your town or city got its name? If you don't know, perhaps you could make up an interesting pretend story that explains the name.

2. The Greeks worshipped Athena as the goddess of wisdom, weaving, and war. We think of owls as wise today because statues of Athena often carried owls in their right hands. Poseidon was god of the sea. What do you think of the behavior of Athena and Poseidon? Do they seem better or worse than human beings, or about the same? In what way does Athena seem wise and in what way not?

3. The ancient Greeks thought that the horse and the olive tree were wonderful gifts from the gods. Can you name an animal and a type of tree that Americans might consider most beautiful or most useful? Explain your answer.

Lesson 5: Dialogue—A Greek Myth

Go Deeper—

1. Ancient people told myths to explain the beginning of things. In this myth, *Athena Defeats Poseidon*, we learn about three beginnings. Circle all three.
   a. the creation of horses
   b. the creation of sheep
   c. the creation of the maple tree
   d. the creation of the olive tree
   e. the origin of the name "Athens"
   f. the origin of the name "Greece"

2. Athena and Poseidon quarreled over the honor of naming Athens after themselves. What word best describes the gods in this myth? Explain your answer in the space below.

   awesome   beautiful   proud   generous

   _____

   _____

   _____

   _____

3. At last, the god and goddess came up with a way to resolve their differences. The verb "resolve" comes from the Latin word *resolvere* which means "to loosen, undo, or settle." Because the two gods stopped quarreling after they resolved their differences, the word "resolve" probably means:
   a. To settle or find a solution to
   b. To halt or stop
   c. To insult or get louder
   d. To make perfect peace

Use the word "resolve" in your own complete sentence.

_____

_____

_____

Writing Time—

1. **COPYWORK**—Notice how this sentence contains a list of items divided by commas. Neatly copy the sentence in the space provided:

   Olive oil could be used to fuel lamps, to make soap, to soothe sunburns, and to clean wounds.

   _____

   _____

   _____

   _____

2. **DICTATION**—Your teacher will read a little part of *Athena Defeats Poseidon* back to you. Please listen carefully! After your teacher reads once, he will read slowly again and include the punctuation marks. Your task will be to write down the sentences as your teacher reads them one by one.

   _____

   _____

   _____

   _____

   _____

   _____

Lesson 5: Dialogue—A Greek Myth

3. **SENTENCE PLAY**—<u>Olive oil could be used to fuel lamps, to make soap, to soothe sunburns, and to clean wounds</u>. There are many other things in this world that have many uses—things such as fire and paper. Use the olive oil sentence as a model to create new lists of four items.

a. In a complete sentence, create a list for "fire."

Fire could be used to _____

_____

_____

_____

_____

b. In a complete sentence, create a list for "paper."

_____

_____

_____

_____

_____

4. **COPIOUSNESS**

a. Mark the nouns (3) and verbs (2) in the sentence below. Place an *N* over the nouns and *V* over the verbs. The name "Poseidon" is a special type of noun called a proper noun. A proper noun names a specific person, place, thing, or idea.

Poseidon created the horse to plow fields.

Use synonyms to replace the words you marked and rewrite the sentence. You may keep Poseidon's name the same or you can give him a descriptive name such as "God of the Sea" or the Roman name "Neptune."

_____

_____

_____

b. Rewrite the sentence with a different subject, but keep the same meaning. A subject tells what the sentence is about.

Poseidon created the horse to help plow fields.

SUBJECT = Poseidon

The horse _____

_____

c. In the following section, you will replace nouns and verbs with synonyms, add adjectives, and change the <u>subject</u> to rewrite a simple sentence. Try to come up with six variations, all keeping nearly the same meaning as the original sentence. We've provided some examples for you.

The mountains are lovely at sunset.

SUBJECT = The mountains
Examples:
1. The <u>hills</u> <u>look</u> <u>beautiful</u> in the <u>setting sun</u>.   (Synonyms)
2. The <u>peaks</u> <u>appear</u> <u>pretty</u> at <u>dusk</u>.   (Synonyms)
3. The <u>lofty</u>, <u>blue</u> <u>mountains</u> are lovely at sunset.   (Added adjectives)
4. The mountains are lovely in the <u>cool</u>, <u>quiet</u> sunset.   (Added adjectives)
5. <u>Sunset</u> makes the mountains lovely.   (Changed subject)
6. <u>Twilight</u> fills the mountains with loveliness.   (Changed subject)

Lesson 5: Dialogue—A Greek Myth

1) Mark the nouns (*N*) and verb (*V*) in the sentence below.

The meal gave me much delight.

SUBJECT = The meal

2) Now rewrite the above sentence, using synonyms to replace the nouns and verbs that you marked.

   i. _____

   ii. _____

3) Add adjectives.

   i. _____

   ii. _____

4) Change the subject.

   i. Much delight _____

   ii. I _____

5. **AMPLIFICATION WITH DIALOGUE**—Athena and Poseidon "quarreled and argued and quarreled some more." That means that they had a long fight with words. It would be interesting to know what they said to each other, wouldn't it? The myth would be longer and more interesting with a good dose of conversation or dialogue.

Let's try to make the story *Athena Defeats Poseidon* longer and more interesting—using dialogue.

a. Read the myth *Athena Defeats Poseidon* again (see the following page). You'll notice that the line "The two gods quarreled and argued and quarreled some more" has been taken out. Instead of that line, let's add dialogue. Write your own version of the quarrel between Athena and Poseidon. The following are some questions to consider as you're writing your dialogue:

- Why are Athena and Poseidon arguing?
- What would they say to undermine each other?
- How would the god of the sea boast?
- How would the goddess of wisdom boast?

Dialogue tips:

- Make sure you identify who is speaking by using cues such as *Poseidon said* and *Athena said* or *he said* and *she said*.
- Whenever a different person speaks, always skip down a line and indent.
- Don't forget to surround each speaker's words with quotation marks!
- If you identify the speaker, separate the speaker's name from the dialogue with a comma.

Examples:

Athena said, "My mind is sharp as steel."

"My mind is sharp as steel," Athena said.

"My mind is sharp," Athena said, "as steel."

Athena Defeats Poseidon

Athena and Poseidon both knew that the small fortress town on top of the hill known as the Acropolis would someday be a famous city. Both gods wanted the honor of naming the town. Athena wanted it to be called Athens after herself. Poseidon, on the other hand, liked the sound of his own name much better.

He said, "_____

_____

_____

_____

_____

_____

_____

_____

_____

_____

_____

_____

_____

At last, they came up with a way to resolve their differences. They agreed to give gifts to the people of the town and allow them to decide which god would name the place.

So Poseidon created the horse and gave the people horses to help plow their fields and to carry men into battle. Athena created the olive tree.

Poseidon almost laughed to see a spindly tree contending against his magnificent new creature. And yet the Greeks found the fruit to be delicious—not only the fruit, but its oil as well. Olive oil could be used to fuel lamps, to make soap, to soothe sunburns, and to clean wounds. The wood of the tree could be carved into beautiful furniture.

In the end, the people voted for Athena's gift. To this day, the city surrounding the Acropolis is known as Athens.

b. When you are finished writing the dialogue between Athena and Poseidon, read the whole myth with your new conversation in it. Check to make sure that you have identified the speakers clearly and have used the correct punctuation.

6. <u>WRITE</u> a monologue about Athena's thoughts as she imagines what gift to give the Greek city. Have her think up a few ideas, and then change her mind, before she settles on the olive tree. Remember that a monologue is one person speaking. Athena can be speaking aloud or thinking up ideas in her head.

_____

_____

_____

_____

_____

_____

_____

_____

_____

_____

_____

_____

_____

_____

_____

_____

_____

_____

Lesson 5: Dialogue—A Greek Myth

Speak It—

Read your new version of the myth, with dialogue, aloud. Have one classmate read the voice of Poseidon and the other classmate read the voice of Athena. Consider acting out the dialogue with motions and costumes.

A Note on Proper Elocution

Whether you are reciting a poem or reading a story out loud, you want to speak in such a way that the audience can hear you "loud and clear." The art of speaking skillfully is known as elocution. So, what goes into proper elocution?

First of all, you should make sure you are pronouncing all of your words clearly. This means you are making each word sharp and crisp instead of blending them together and mumbling. You want to say, "To be or not to be, that is the question," with each word separate from the next. You don't want to say, "Tobeornottobethatisthequestion."

Secondly, good posture is very important for speaking loudly enough. You can't breathe very well if you are slouched over. Stand up straight and tall, square your shoulders and look at your audience. Look directly into their eyes. This will help your listeners know that you are a confident speaker. They will enjoy your recitation more when they see how confident you are.

Finally, don't speak too quickly. It's hard to understand a recitation that blasts off like a rocket ship. You will want to speak at a good pace and pause every now and then to let your words sink in.

You will delight your listeners if you can stand up straight, look into their eyes, and speak loud and clear at just the right pace.

Lesson 6

Description— Another Greek Myth

In the previous lesson, in which Athena defeats Poseidon, we learned that conversation can make a story longer and more interesting. Do you remember the name for conversation between two or more characters? How about the name for conversation where one character talks to himself or thinks aloud?

Another way to make a story longer and more interesting is to use <u>description</u>. A writer uses description to help the reader "feel" a story more keenly. It appeals to our five senses: seeing, hearing, touching, tasting, and smelling. In fact, description is so important to storytelling that we have devoted our fifth book in this series to it.

Here is the first paragraph of *The Wolves of Willoughby Chase* by Joan Aiken. Notice how the author changes the mood from cheerful to scary in just a few short sentences:

> It was dusk—winter's dusk. Snow lay white and shining over pleated hills, and icicles hung from forest trees. Snow lay piled on the dark road across Willoughby Wold, but from dawn men had been clearing it with

brooms and shovels. There were hundreds of them at work, wrapped in sacking because of the bitter cold, and keeping together in groups for fear of the wolves, grown savage and reckless from hunger.

What if Joan Aiken had left out all description? The paragraph would read like this:

Men shoveled the snow.

If you ask me, that's pretty boring! What a difference description makes in raising our interest in a story!

Description is most effective when it's neither too sparse nor too dense. It's often said that Victorian fiction, such as that by Charles Dickens, would be better if chopped by a good editor. On the other hand, modern fiction is sometimes so lacking in description that it comes off as sterile. Description should be an active part of the story, adding richness and interest to action and to dialogue. For example, " 'That's a lovely painting,' he said," might be improved this way: " 'That's a colorful Van Gogh,' he gasped and then coughed, choking on his morning coffee and spewing it all over the priceless painting."

Here's another example of rich description adapted from the novel *Peter Pan*—a description of Captain Hook:

In the midst of the pirates reclined James Hook. He lay at his ease in a rough chariot drawn and pushed by his men, and instead of a right hand he had the iron hook with which he encouraged them to increase their pace. As dogs this terrible man treated and addressed them, and as dogs they obeyed him. In person he looked thin and dark-faced, and his hair was dressed in long curls, which at a little distance looked like black candles, and gave a singularly threatening expression to his handsome **countenance**. His eyes were of the blue of the forget-me-not, and of a profound sadness, except when he was plunging his hook into you, at which time two red spots appeared in them and lit them up horribly.

It would have been far easier for author James Barrie to write merely:

Captain Hook was a fierce man and treated his men badly.

How sad it would be to have such a weak, dull picture of the captain!

What about description in mythology? I'm sorry to report that description in most myths is pretty thin. When we hear about Athena, the best we get is "gray-eyed Athena" or "bright-eyed Athena" and sometimes "lovely-haired goddess." That's not much to go on. Let's read another myth about Athena and see if we can't improve the description. This time, the goddess shows herself to be quite severe with a mortal woman who dares to mock her.

The Greek word for "spider" is *arachne*, which comes from the name of the weaving woman in this myth. Even today, scientists refer to the family of animals that includes spiders as *Arachnida*. When someone is afraid of spiders (and/or possibly other members of this family, such as scorpions), she is said to have <u>arachnophobia</u>.

The nymphs in this story are lowly goddesses who inhabit the forests and streams.

Athena and Arachne

Adapted from Thomas Bulfinch, *The Age of Fable*

Once there was a mortal woman who dared to compete with Athena. This mortal was Arachne, a maiden so skilled at weaving that even the forest nymphs and water nymphs came to stare at her carpets. "I am such an amazing weaver," said Arachne to the nymphs, "that not even Athena could do better. Why, it would be an easy thing for me to beat her in a weaving contest."

Of course, sooner or later, this boast reached the ears of the goddess. Athena was none too pleased when she heard such frightful immodesty. Taking the disguise of an old woman, the goddess hobbled up to Arachne's **loom**.

"You are indeed very skilled," Athena said. "Challenge your fellow mortals as you will, but don't compete with an **immortal** goddess. Instead, I advise you to ask her for her forgiveness. Perhaps she will pardon you."

Arachne stopped her spinning and stared at the old woman with anger in her eyes. "I'm not afraid of the goddess. Let her try her skill against mine. Let her come! She won't dare."

Lesson 6: Description—Another Greek Myth

"She comes," said Athena. Dropping her disguise, the goddess stood bold and bright before Arachne. All the nymphs bowed low. All the mortals ran away. Arachne alone sat shamelessly on her stool.

Athena did not waste her words again, but immediately took her seat at a loom. "Let the contest begin!" And so both women worked away with speed.

On her carpet, Athena created the scene of her contest with Poseidon. All the gods of Olympus, including the mountain itself, were woven into the background. Such a dazzling work of skill and beauty had never been seen on earth before. But Arachne did amazing work as well. She wove scenes of the gods making fools of themselves. So realistic were the figures that they seemed almost alive.

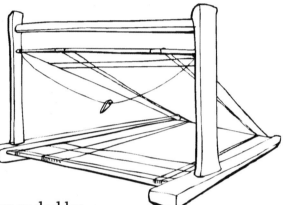

When Athena saw such wicked pictures, she lost her temper. She struck the loom with her **shuttle** and it fell to pieces. Then she touched the forehead of Arachne and made her feel guilt and shame. The mortal woman suddenly realized the error of her ways and, running out of her house, she hung herself by the neck.

Athena pitied the poor woman as she saw her suspended by a rope. "Live," she said, "guilty woman! Preserve the memory of this lesson, both you and your children, to all future times." Immediately Arachne's body shrank up and her head grew smaller yet. Her fingers stuck to her side and served as legs. And now it is possible to see the children of Arachne still hanging suspended by threads and weaving webs, for the children of Arachne are all spiders.

Tell It Back—Narration

1. **ORAL NARRATION**—Without looking at the myth, tell back *Athena and Arachne* as best as you can remember it using your own words and any words from the story, including "loom." For extra practice, record your telling back into your favorite device and play it afterwards.

   • Keep the events of the story in their proper order.

Lesson 6: Description—Another Greek Myth

Here is the first sentence to get you started:

Once there was a mortal woman who dared to compete with Athena.

2. Put the events in order below using *B* for beginning, *M* for middle, and *E* for end.

_____ "I am such an amazing weaver," said Arachne to the nymphs, "that not even Athena could do better."

_____ Athena pitied the poor woman. "Live," she said, "guilty woman! Preserve the memory of this lesson, both you and your children, to all future times."

_____ Athena did not waste her words again, but immediately took her seat at a loom. "Let the contest begin!"

3. **WRITTEN NARRATION**

a. Write your own sentence to tell what happens at the <u>beginning</u> of the story.

_____

_____

_____

b. Write your own sentence to tell what happens in the <u>middle</u> of the story.

_____

_____

_____

c. Write your own sentence to tell what happens at the <u>end</u> of the story.

_____

_____

_____

Talk About It—

1. If there were a moral for this myth, what might it be? Remember from *Writing & Rhetoric: Fable* that a moral is a short truth or proverb.

2. Why do you suppose Athena was so angry with Arachne? Which of the women do you think was the better weaver?

3. Have you ever bragged that you were better at something than an older brother or sister, or even an adult? Why did you do it? What happened after you bragged?

Go Deeper—

1. Athena was a goddess, one of the immortals of Mount Olympus. An "immortal" person cannot die, but rather lives forever. Arachne was not a goddess; she was an ordinary woman—a mortal woman. The word "mortal" probably means:

   a. She can die.

   b. She is lazy.

   c. She is weak.

   d. She is powerful.

2. Ancient people told myths to explain the beginning of things. In this myth, *Athena and Arachne*, we learn about the beginning of what?

   a. weaving

   b. spiders

   c. looms

   d. wisdom

3. Why do you think this myth was told in Ancient Greece?

   a. To show that bragging is rude.

   b. To make people feel sorry for spiders.

   c. To prove that people are better weavers than goddesses.

   d. To warn mortal people not to challenge the gods.

4. Athena and Arachne are the main characters in this myth. Only one of these characters changes. A changeable character is known as a **dynamic character**. We are rarely interested in stories in which nobody learns a lesson or in which everything goes along just as it did before. People change in response to the stress and challenges of life. Ants and lizards do not change. Which character is the dynamic character in *Athena and Arachne*? How does she change?

_____

_____

_____

_____

_____

_____

Writing Time—

1. **COPYWORK**—Neatly copy the sentence in the space provided:
Dropping her disguise, the goddess stood bold and bright before Arachne.

_____

_____

_____

_____

2. **DICTATION**—Your teacher will read a little part of *Athena and Arachne* back to you. Please listen carefully! After your teacher reads once, he will read slowly again and include the punctuation marks. Your task will be to write down the sentences as your teacher reads them one by one.

_____

_____

_____

_____

_____

_____

3. **SENTENCE PLAY**—<u>Dropping her disguise, the goddess stood bold and bright before Arachne</u>. Notice how two things are happening at the same time in this sentence. What are those two things?

   a. Using this sentence as a model, tell us what could have happened if Athena had dropped a bowling ball on her foot.

      Example: *Dropping the bowling ball on her foot, Athena revealed her clumsiness.*

      Dropping _____

      _____

      _____

   b. Tell us what could have happened if Athena had kicked a field goal.

      Kicking _____

      _____

      _____

   c. Tell us what could have happened if Athena had eaten a bowl of broccoli.

      Eating _____

      _____

      _____

4. **COPIOUSNESS**—Mark the nouns (3) and verbs (2) in the following sentence. Place an *N* over the nouns and *V* over the verbs. Replace nouns and verbs with synonyms, add adjectives, and change the <u>subject</u> to rewrite the simple sentence below. Try to come up with five variations, all keeping nearly the same meaning as the original sentence. You may keep Athena's name the same or you can give her a descriptive name such as "goddess of wisdom" or the Roman name "Minerva."

The pictures made Athena lose her temper.

SUBJECT = The pictures

Replace nouns and verbs with synonyms. You can replace the word "pictures" with the synonyms "illustrations" and "images."

a. _____

Add adjectives to describe the nouns.

b. _____

c. _____

Change the <u>subject</u>.

d. _____

e. _____

5. **DIALOGUE**—There is plenty of conversation in *Athena and Arachne*. This conversation makes the myth more interesting, doesn't it?

Go back to the myth on pages 65–66 and use two colors of highlighter pen to mark the conversation in *Athena and Arachne*. Athena can be yellow, for instance, and Arachne can be pink.

6. **AMPLIFICATION WITH DESCRIPTION**—There is very little description in Athena and Arachne. For example, we don't know what Arachne's house looks like. Is it made of brick or wood? We don't know what it feels like either. Is it cool and damp inside or hot and dry? We don't know what it smells like. Does it smell of olive oil and parsley or of pistachio nuts and honey? And what sounds can be heard outside? Can Arachne hear seagulls squawking or dogs barking or donkeys braying?

We don't know what the main characters, Athena and Arachne, look like. Myth makers tell us that Athena always wore the full battle armor she was born with. She is pictured as having gray eyes, a stern look to her face, and long, flowing hair. Is that how you see Athena?

Now picture Athena in disguise as an old lady. What does she look like without the battle armor? Perhaps she holds a cane instead of a spear. What does she wear? How does she walk? Imagine the features of her body. What do her hands and feet look like? What about her nose and eyes, her ears and skin? Imagine the look on her face. What kind of expression is she wearing?

In the myth below, insert your description of the old lady (Athena in disguise) in the space provided.

Once there was a mortal woman who dared to compete with Athena. This mortal was Arachne, a maiden so skilled at weaving that even the forest nymphs and water nymphs came to stare at her carpets. "I am such an amazing weaver," said Arachne to the nymphs, "that not even Athena could do better. Why, it would be an easy thing for me to beat her in a weaving contest."

Of course, sooner or later, this boast reached the ears of the goddess. Athena was none too pleased when she heard such frightful immodesty. Taking the disguise of an old woman, the goddess hobbled up to Arachne's loom.

_____

_____

_____

_____

_____

_____

_____

_____

_____

_____

_____

_____

_____

_____

_____

_____

_____

_____

_____

_____

"You are indeed very skilled," Athena said. "Challenge your fellow mortals as you will, but don't compete with an immortal goddess. Instead, I advise you to ask her for her forgiveness. Perhaps she will pardon you."

Arachne stopped her spinning and stared at the old woman with anger in her eyes. "I'm not afraid of the goddess. Let her try her skill against mine. Let her come! She won't dare."

Now read the story above with your description included. Why does your description make the narrative more interesting?

Speak It—

Research a type of spider—such as the wolf spider, the brown recluse spider, the black widow spider, the mouse spider, or the trapdoor spider. Write interesting facts in complete sentences on note cards, one fact per card. Make sure you include facts such as: habitat (where the spider lives), diet (what the spider eats), hunting (how the spider catches its food), and toxicity (how poisonous the spider is). Use the note cards and your own illustration to tell your class about the spider. Or you can record your telling into your favorite device and play it back.[1]

---

1. To review the elocution instructions, see page 129.

Lesson 6: Description—Another Greek Myth

Lesson 7 ···

Combining Dialogue and Description, Part I

You are about to read a narrative of one of the most famous battles in history, the Battle of Thermopylae. The fierce clash happened in the narrow passage between two mountain cliffs known as the Hot Gates. On one side stood the Greeks, who were defending their land and homes from a massive invasion; on the other side attacked the Persians, a huge army determined to crush Greece and take it over. Eventually, the small force of Greeks was defeated, but not before they inflicted terrible losses on the invaders. Not long after Thermopylae, the giant Persian navy and army was mopped up by the Greeks in the Battles of Salamis and Plataea.

For those of you who enjoy tales of courage and daring, this narrative is much too brief. You can help improve it by adding dialogue and description.

The Brave 300

Adapted from James Baldwin, *Fifty Famous Stories Retold*

All Greece was in danger. A mighty army, led by the great king of Persia, had come from the east. It was marching along the seashore, and in a few days would be in Greece. The Persian king, Xerxes, had sent messengers into every city and state, demanding water and earth as **tokens** that the land and the sea belonged to him. But the Greeks said, "No! We will be free."

And so there was a great stir throughout Greece. The men armed themselves and made haste to go out and drive back their foe. The women, as brave as the men, stayed behind to protect their homes and to dry their children's tears.

There was only one way by which the Persian army could go into Greece on the eastern side, and that was by the narrow pass of Thermopylae between the mountains and the sea. Leonidas, the king of the Spartans, guarded this pass with 300 Spartan soldiers. Soon the Persian soldiers were seen coming. There were so many of them that no man could count them. How could a handful of men hope to stand against so great a host?

Lesson 7: *Combining Dialogue and Description, Part 1*

And yet Leonidas and his Spartans held their ground. They had made up their minds to die at their post. A Persian messenger said, "Surrender! There are so many of us that our arrows darken the sun."

"So much the better," said the Spartans. "We will fight in the shade."

Bravely they stood in the narrow pass. Bravely they faced their foes. To the Spartans, there was no such thing as fear. The Persians came forward, only to meet death at the points of Greek spears. Each time the Persians were driven back, King Xerxes leapt from his throne in despair.

But one by one the Spartans fell. At last their spears were broken; yet still they stood side by side, fighting to the last. Some fought with swords, some with daggers, and some with only their fists and teeth.

All day long, the army of the Persians was kept at bay. But when the sun went down, there was not one Spartan left alive. Where they had stood, there was only a heap of the slain, all bristled over with spears and arrows.

Twenty thousand Persian soldiers had fallen before that handful of Greek men. Not enough were left to take over the country they were invading. And so Greece was saved.

Thousands of years have passed since then; but men still like to tell the story of Leonidas and the brave 300 who died for their country's sake.

Tell It Back—Narration

1. **ORAL NARRATION**—Without looking at the myth, tell back *The Brave 300* as best as you can remember it using your own words and words from the story. For further practice, you can record your telling back into your favorite device and play it afterwards.

   • Keep the events of the story in their proper order.

   Here are the first two sentences to get you started:

   All Greece was in danger. A mighty army, led by the great king of Persia, had come from the east.

2. Put the events in order below using *B* for beginning, *M* for middle, and *E* for end.

_____ All Greece was in danger. A mighty army, led by the great king of Persia, had come from the east. It was marching along the seashore, and in a few days would be in Greece.

_____ Bravely they stood in the narrow pass. Bravely they faced their foes. To the Spartans, there was no such thing as fear. The Persians came forward, only to meet death at the points of Greek spears.

_____ Twenty thousand Persian soldiers had fallen before that handful of men. And so Greece was saved.

3. **WRITTEN NARRATION**

a. Write your own sentence to tell what happens at the <u>beginning</u> of the story.

_____

_____

_____

b. Write your own sentence to tell what happens in the <u>middle</u> of the story.

_____

_____

_____

c. Write your own sentence to tell what happens at the <u>end</u> of the story.

_____

_____

_____

Talk About It—

1. "Not one Spartan was left alive." When a group of soldiers fights heroically to the death, we call it a last stand. Why do you think the Spartans chose to die in a last stand rather than give up and surrender?

2. The Persian king, Xerxes, was famous for his fits of rage. He had his workers build a bridge over a wide river, the Hellespont, to help his army march into Greece. Fortunately for the Greeks, a storm came along and destroyed the bridge. In his anger, Xerxes ordered his soldiers to whip the water with ropes and brand it with hot irons. He also had them taunt the river, calling it names like "bitter water" and "treacherous stream." Finally, he ordered the heads cut off of some of the men who built the bridge. What does this story show about the character of Xerxes? Would you want Xerxes to be your ruler? Why not?

3. Look carefully at the statue of Leonidas at Thermopylae for a minute, then close your eyes. How would you describe the warrior as you see the statue in your mind? What is he wearing? What is he holding in his hands? What is his attitude? Can you stand in the same pose?

Go Deeper—

1. What kind of narrative do you think *The Brave 300* is?
   a. parable
   b. myth
   c. fairy tale
   d. history

2. Because the Persian king wanted to own all of Greece, he demanded tokens of earth and water. These tokens were meant to say, "You can take over as ruler of Greece and nobody will fight you." The word "tokens" here means:

    a. signs of surrender

    b. rides on a subway

    c. speeches of victory

    d. spears of war

3. "Soon the Persian soldiers were seen coming. There were so many of them that no man could count them. How could a handful of men hope to stand against so great a host?" What is the meaning of the word "host" in this sentence?

    a. a huge army

    b. a hotel manager

    c. a crowd of people

    d. a million soldiers

4. In this story, which weapon did the Greeks first use to hold the Persians back

    a. swords

    b. daggers

    c. spears

    d. fists and teeth

Writing Time—

1. **COPYWORK**—Neatly copy the sentence in the space provided:

A mighty army, led by the great king of Persia, had come from the east.

_____

_____

_____

Lesson 7: Combining Dialogue and Description, Part 1

2. **DICTATION**—Your teacher will read a little part of *The Brave 300* back to you. Please listen carefully! After your teacher reads once, he will read slowly again and include the punctuation marks. Your task will be to write down the sentences as your teacher reads them one by one.

_____

_____

_____

_____

_____

_____

3. **SENTENCE PLAY**—<u>There were so many Persians that their arrows darkened the sun</u>. Using this sentence as a model, write two more sentences to show the enormous size of the Persian army. The following are some possible ways to start your sentences:

There were so many Persians that their shields . . .

There were so many Persians that their spears . . .

There were so many Persians that their footsteps . . .

a. _____

_____

b. _____

_____

4. **COPIOUSNESS**—Mark the nouns (3) and verb (1) in the sentence below. Place an *N* over the nouns and *V* over the verb. Replace nouns and the verb with synonyms, add adjectives, and change the <u>subject</u> to rewrite the simple sentence below. Try to come up with five variations, all keeping nearly the same meaning as the original sentence.

Our soldiers will fight the battle in the shade.

SUBJECT = Soldiers

Replace nouns and verbs with synonyms.

a. _____

Add adjectives to describe the nouns.

b. _____

c. _____

Change the subject.

d. Shade _____

e. The battle _____

5. **AMPLIFICATION WITH DIALOGUE**—<u>The women, as brave as the</u>
<u>men, stayed behind to protect their homes and to dry their children's tears</u>.
Remember that conversation can make a story more interesting. Write a dialogue between the children and their mothers. What are the children afraid of? What can their mothers say to comfort them? Insert your conversation into the story.

The men armed themselves and made haste to go out and drive back their foe. The women, as brave as the men, stayed behind to protect their homes and to dry their children's tears.

One girl asked her mother . . .
One boy said to his mother . . .

_____

_____

_____

_____

_____

_____

_____

_____

_____

_____

_____

6. **AMPLIFICATION WITH DESCRIPTION**—<u>Soon the Persian soldiers were seen coming. There were so many of them that no man could count them.</u> Describe what the Persian host might have looked like from high on the mountain. Be sure to appeal to the senses: sight, sound, touch, taste, and smell. Add this description when you re-read the story.

Soon the Persian soldiers were seen coming. There were so many of them that no man could count them.

_____

_____

_____

_____

_____

_____

_____

_____

_____

_____

_____

_____

_____

_____

_____

_____

Speak It—

One of the most famous **epitaphs** of all time was written by the ancient Greek poet Simonides for the brave Spartans who died at Thermopylae. What is an "epitaph"? It is a line or two on a grave marker that serves as a reminder of the dead person or people buried below. In Greek, Simonides' epitaph looks like this:

**Ὦ ξεῖν', ἀγγέλλειν Λακεδαιμονίοις ὅτι τῇδε
κείμεθα, τοῖς κείνων ῥήμασι πειθόμενοι**

These lines have been translated many, many different ways. You can see the flexibility of the English language just by reading the many different and copious translations. Your teacher will assign you a translation to memorize. Perhaps each of you can stand up and present these bold words in a rapid chain of recitations.

Go, tell the Spartans, you who read this stone
That we lie here, and that their will was done.

Go, wayfarer, bear news to Sparta's town

that here, their bidding done, we laid us down. —Cyril E. Robinson

Go, stranger, and to Spartans tell

That here, obeying her behests, we fell. —George Rawlinson

Go tell the Spartans, thou who passest by,

That, faithful to their precepts, here we lie. —William Lisle Bowles

Go tell the Spartans, stranger passing by,

That here, obedient to their laws, we lie. —Steven Pressfield

Friend, tell the Spartans that on this hill

We lie obedient to them still. —Michael Dodson

Stranger! To Sparta say, her faithful band

Here lie in death, remembering her command. —Frances Hodgson

When you visit Sparta, tell them,

Here, the soldiers kept their word. —Simonides

Stranger, go tell the Spartans that here,

obeying their orders, we died.

Stranger, tell the Spartans that we behaved

as they would wish us to, and are buried here. —William Golding

Stranger, announce to the Spartans that you found us here

Resting in peace, their decrees being upheld and obeyed.

Remember the importance of elocution, which is the art of speaking skillfully! As a speaker you will want to stand up straight, look into the eyes of your audience, and speak loud and clear. Make sure you don't speak too quickly, and pause every now and then to let your words sink in. See the complete elocution instructions on page 129.

Lesson 8

Combining Dialogue and Description, Part 2

The Romans loved almost everything about Greece. They loved the way Greeks dressed and the way Greeks built their temples and the way Greeks ran their government. They loved Greece so much that they decided to take it over and make it part of Rome. But a strange thing happened after the Romans conquered Greece—the Romans started to look and act more like Greeks themselves. They borrowed the look of Greek buildings. They borrowed the look of Greek art. They even borrowed Greek gods and goddesses. As the saying goes, "Rome may have conquered Greece, but Greece conquered Rome."

The Romans loved Greek poems as well. They wanted to blend their history with the glorious stories told by Homer in the *Iliad* and the *Odyssey*. So a Roman poet named Virgil wrote a new poem—the *Aeneid*—and told the story of Aeneas, a Trojan hero.

When Troy was destroyed by the Greeks, Virgil tells us that Aeneas, son of the goddess Aphrodite, managed to escape death. With a band of faithful followers, he set sail and eventually landed in Italy. There he married the princess of a kingdom known as Latium, the land of the Latins. Can you guess what language was spoken in Latium? Aeneas and the princess Lavinia had many children, grandchildren, and great-grandchildren. Here is the story of their great-great-great-great-great-grand-daughter, Rhea Silvia, and her two famous sons.

Romulus and Remus

Rhea Silvia was born a princess of Latium, but for a princess she lived a difficult life. When she was a young girl, about six or seven years old, her wicked uncle Amulius drove her father, the king, from his throne and took over the kingdom.

Amulius forced Rhea Silvia to become a priestess in a temple of the goddess Vesta. These priestesses were never permitted to get married or to have children. Uncle Amulius did not want Rhea Silvia to have any children that would overthrow him the way he had overthrown her father. Poor Rhea Silvia! Her job in the temple was to keep an altar fire burning all day and all night, as long as she lived. Because of her uncle's wickedness, she would never have a family of her own.

One day Rhea Silvia happened to be walking through the forest toward the temple of Mars, the war god. A wolf sprang out of the bushes and attacked her. She might have been killed if a man in armor hadn't rushed to her rescue. The warrior killed the wolf with one stroke of his sword. Rhea Silvia recognized him as the god Mars himself.

Even though she was not permitted to have children, Rhea Silvia secretly bore two sons for Mars—twin boys! When Uncle Amulius learned that Rhea Silvia had given birth, he flew into a rage. "She has betrayed me," he said to himself. "She is trying to steal the throne using her two sons. But I will never allow that to happen!"

Amulius turned to one of his servants. "Throw the brats into the river Tiber!" he shouted. "Let them drown."

Now, the servant was a kindhearted man, a shepherd by the name of Faustulus. He could not **stomach**[1] the thought of murdering two helpless babes. So he placed them in a little boat and set them adrift on the river Tiber. "Perhaps someone will come along to help them," he said hopefully.

The boat drifted along, now spinning in circles, now bouncing over rough water, until at last it was thrown upon the shore. The two babies tumbled out onto the green grass. A mother wolf heard them crying and came out of her den to investigate. Rather than devouring the twins, the wolf carried them back to her home in the rocks. She nursed them and licked them and kept them warm at night with her own body. A woodpecker also helped the boys by bringing them nuts and berries to eat.

No one knows for sure how long the brothers lived in the forest. When they were still toddlers, Faustulus found them again and took them home to live in his shepherd's hut. Faustulus raised the boys as if they were his own sons, giving them the names Romulus and Remus.

As the boys grew older, they learned from Faustulus that they were noble princes and not shepherd boys at all. Of course, once Romulus and Remus heard this news it was hard for them to remain content being mere shepherds. Together they raised an army against their granduncle, the wicked Amulius. Most people in the kingdom of

---

1. Remember, you can find the definitions for bolded words in the glossary at the back of the book.

Lesson 8: Combining Dialogue and Description, Part 2

Latium were heartily sick of the **tyrant** king and welcomed the revolt. Romulus and Remus stormed the palace and killed Amulius as he was running out of the throne room.

Perhaps Romulus and Remus are most famous for what they did next. Together they returned to the Tiber River, where Faustulus had pushed them into the water, and on its banks and in the surrounding hills, they built a new city. That city grew to be the most powerful, most beautiful, most amazing city in its day. Can you guess its name? The city of Rome was named after the Latin prince Romulus.

Tell It Back—Narration

1. **ORAL NARRATION**—Without looking at the myth, tell back *Romulus and Remus* as best as you can remember it using your own words and words from the story. For further practice, you could record it on your favorite device and play it afterwards.

   • Keep the events of the story in their proper order.

   ## Here are the first two sentences to get you started:

   Rhea Silvia was born a princess of Latium, but for a princess she lived a difficult life. When she was a young girl, about six or seven years old, her wicked uncle Amulius drove her father, the king, from his throne and took over the kingdom.

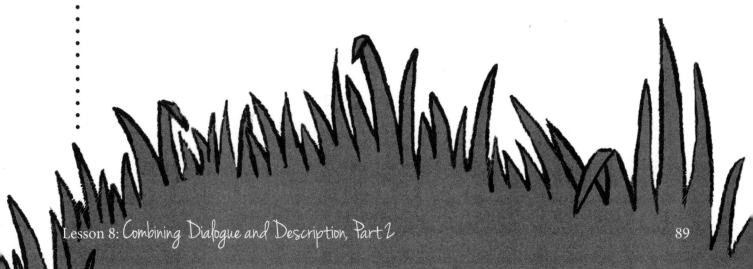

2. Put the events in order below using *B* for beginning and *E* for end. There are two passages here from the middle of the story. Use *M1* for the first middle passage and *M2* for the second middle passage.

_____ One day Rhea Silvia happened to be walking through the forest toward the temple of Mars, the war god. A wolf sprang out of the bushes and attacked her.

_____ Romulus and Remus stormed the palace and killed Amulius as he was running out of the throne room.

_____ When Rhea Silvia was a young girl, about six or seven years old, her wicked uncle Amulius drove her father, the king, from his throne.

_____ The servant placed the twin babies in a little boat and set them adrift on the river Tiber.

3. **WRITTEN NARRATION**

a. Write your own sentence to tell what happens at the <u>beginning</u> of the story.

_____

_____

_____

b. Write your own sentence to tell what happens in the <u>middle</u> of the story.

_____

_____

_____

c. Write your own sentence to tell what happens at the <u>end</u> of the story.

_____

_____

_____

Lesson 8: Combining Dialogue and Description, Part 2

Talk About It—

1. Would you like to have an identical twin? Why or why not?

2. What parts of this story seem real and what parts seem make-believe? You might want to use two different highlighters to mark the sentences before you answer.

3. Look carefully at the print of Peter Paul Rubens's *Romulus and Remus*. What characters from the story do you recognize? Why do you suppose they are all smiling and happy? The man reclining on the left is Tiberinus, the god of the river Tiber. Why do you suppose Rubens included him in his painting?

4. Look carefully at the statue of the *Capitoline She-wolf* for a minute or two, then close your eyes. How would you describe the wolf as you see the statue in your mind? What is the expression on her face? What are the baby boys doing?

Go Deeper—

1. What kind of narrative do you think *Romulus and Remus* is to us today?
   a. parable
   b. myth
   c. fairy tale
   d. history

2. What kind of narrative do you think *Romulus and Remus* was to the ancient Romans?

    a. parable

    b. myth

    c. fairy tale

    d. history

3. In *Romulus and Remus*, we learn about the beginning of what?

    a. the fear of wolves

    b. the city of Rome

    c. the river Tiber

    d. the worship of Vesta

4. In *Romulus and Remus*, we learn that the Romans are related to the great Trojan hero Aeneas through Rhea Silvia. We also learn that they are related to the war god Mars. What do you think was the main reason this story was told in Ancient Rome?

    a. to make Romans feel proud of their family history

    b. to help Romans be less afraid of wolves

    c. to warn Romans against wicked kings

    d. to show that twin babies are better than one baby

5. The kind shepherd could not stomach the thought of murdering two helpless babes. In this sentence, the word "stomach" does not mean belly. It means that the servant could not bear the thought of killing

babies. In other words, the thought was sickening to him. Circle the word that expresses the same idea.

The kind shepherd could not _____ the thought of murdering two helpless babes.

a. skip

b. forget

c. stand

d. remember

6. A hungry wolf might have **devoured** the two babies. To "devour" means to eat greedily. Give two reasons why the mother wolf might not have eaten the babies.

a. _____

_____

b. _____

_____

7. Because King Amulius steals the throne and treats his family terribly, the word "tyrant" probably means:

a. a wise ruler

b. a fearless ruler

c. a foolish ruler

d. a cruel ruler

8. Did you notice the word "revolt" in the story? According to the author, most of the people of Latium welcomed the revolt against King Amulius. "Revolt" comes from the Latin verb *revolvere*, which means "to turn or roll back." Use a dictionary to write the definition of "revolt" in the space below and then use it in a complete sentence that shows its meaning.

Definition _____

_____

Sentence _____

_____

Writing Time—

1. **COPYWORK**—Neatly copy the sentence in the space provided:

   As the boys grew older, they learned that they were noble princes and not shepherd boys at all.

   _____

   _____

   _____

2. **DICTATION**—Your teacher will read a little part of *Romulus and Remus* back to you. Please listen carefully! After your teacher reads once, she will read slowly again and include the punctuation marks. Your task will be to write down the sentences as your teacher reads them one by one.

   _____

   _____

   _____

   _____

   _____

   _____

   _____

   _____

   _____

Lesson 8: Combining Dialogue and Description, Part 2

3. **SENTENCE PLAY**—<u>Because of her uncle's wickedness, Rhea Silvia would never have a family of her own</u>. Notice how one thing leads to another in this sentence. The uncle's wickedness leads to Rhea Silvia not having a family of her own. The word "because" is like glue joining one thing to the other. Because cheese stinks, you shouldn't keep it in your pocket. Because birds have wings and feathers, they can fly. Finish these other "because" sentences.

a. Because my pencil broke,

_____

_____

b. Because of the loud party next door,

_____

_____

c. Because the snow is coming down hard,

_____

_____

d. Because _____

_____

4. **COPIOUSNESS:**

Mark the nouns (3) and verb (1) in the sentence below. Place an *N* over the nouns and *V* over the verbs. Replace nouns and verbs with synonyms, add adjectives, and change the <u>subject</u> to rewrite the simple sentence below. Try to come up with five variations, all keeping nearly the same meaning as the original sentence.

Rhea Silvia cared for the fire in the temple.

SUBJECT = Rhea Silvia

Replace nouns and verbs with synonyms. You don't need to change the proper noun "Rhea Silvia," but you could call her by a synonymous description such as "the great-granddaughter of Aeneas."

a. _____

_____

_____

Add adjectives.

b. _____

_____

_____

c. _____

_____

_____

Change the subject.

d. The fire _____

_____

_____

e. The temple _____

_____

_____

5. DIALOGUE AND MONOLOGUE

a. Read the narrative *Romulus and Remus* again. Or you could play back the audio recording you made, or use the recording from Classical Academic Press.

b. Do you remember that dialogue is a conversation between two or more people? Monologue is a conversation that a person has with herself, all alone. Use a highlighter pen to mark the two monologues in *Romulus and Remus*. Use a different color highlighter to mark the dialogue.

6. AMPLIFICATION WITH DIALOGUE AND DESCRIPTION

In <u>Section A</u>, write a dialogue between the tyrant King Amulius and the kindly shepherd Faustulus. What could Faustulus say to King Amulius to try to stop him from killing the twin boys? What would the wicked king say in reply? In <u>Section B</u>, write a description of the wolf and her behavior. What was the look on her face? What does the wolf do when she first sees the boys?

Romulus and Remus

Rhea Silvia was born a princess of Latium, but for a princess she lived a difficult life. When she was a young girl, about six or seven years old, her wicked uncle Amulius drove her father, the king, from his throne and took over the kingdom.

Amulius forced Rhea Silvia to become a priestess in a temple of the goddess Vesta. These priestesses were never permitted to get married or to have children. Uncle Amulius did not want Rhea Silvia to have any children that would overthrow him the way he had overthrown her father. Poor Rhea Silvia! Her job in the temple was to keep an altar fire burning all day and all night, as long as she lived. Because of her uncle's wickedness, she would never have a family of her own.

One day Rhea Silvia happened to be walking through the forest toward the temple of Mars, the war god. A wolf sprang out of the bushes and attacked her.

She might have been killed if a man in armor hadn't rushed to her rescue. The warrior killed the wolf with one stroke of his sword. Rhea Silvia recognized him as the god Mars himself.

Even though she was not permitted to have children, Rhea Silvia secretly bore two sons for Mars—twin boys! When Uncle Amulius learned that Rhea Silvia had given birth, he flew into a rage. "She has betrayed me," he said to himself. "She is trying to steal the throne using her two sons. But I will never allow that to happen!"

Amulius turned to one of his servants. "Throw the brats into the river Tiber!" he shouted. "Let them drown."

Now the servant was a kindhearted man, a shepherd by the name of Faustulus. He could not stomach the thought of murdering two helpless babes.

Section A

Bowing low, he said to the king,

_____

_____

_____

_____

_____

_____

_____

_____

_____

_____

_____

Lesson 8: *Combining Dialogue and Description, Part 2*

Knowing it was hopeless to try to change the king's mind, Faustulus placed the boys in a little boat and set them adrift on the river Tiber. "Perhaps someone will come along to help them," he said hopefully.

The boat drifted along, now spinning in circles, now bouncing over rough water, until at last it was thrown upon the shore. The two babies tumbled out onto the green grass. A mother wolf heard them crying and came out of her den to investigate.

Section B

She . . .

_____

_____

_____

_____

_____

_____

_____

_____

_____

_____

_____

_____

And the story continues...

Rather than devouring the twins, the wolf carried them back to her home in the rocks. She nursed them and licked them and kept them warm at night with her own body. A woodpecker also helped the boys by bringing them nuts and berries to eat.

No one knows for sure how long the brothers lived in the forest. When they were still toddlers, Faustulus found them again and took them home to live in his shepherd's hut. Faustulus raised the boys as if they were his own sons, giving them the names Romulus and Remus.

As the boys grew older, they learned from Faustulus that they were noble princes and not shepherd boys at all. Of course, once Romulus and Remus heard this news it was hard for them to remain content being mere shepherds. Together they raised an army against their granduncle, the wicked Amulius. Most people in the kingdom of Latium were heartily sick of the tyrant king and welcomed the revolt. Romulus and Remus stormed the palace and killed Amulius as he was running out of the throne room.

Perhaps Romulus and Remus are most famous for what they did next. Together they returned to the Tiber River, where Faustulus had pushed them into the water, and on its banks and in the surrounding hills they built a new city. That city grew to be the most powerful, most beautiful, most amazing city in its day. Can you guess its name? The city of Rome was named after the Latin prince Romulus.

Speak It—

Read aloud your expanded version of *Romulus and Remus* to a partner or recording device (and listen to your recording).

Lesson 9

Conflict—
The Middle of the Story

For many authors, the hardest part of writing a story is the middle. Once you have a beginning, it's usually pretty easy to see the ending.

▶ If you write a story about a girl meeting a stray dog, what might be a happy ending? What might be a sad ending?

▶ If you write a story about a boy who discovers a treasure chest buried in his backyard, what might be a happy ending? What might be a sad ending?

The <u>beginning</u> of the story is all about grabbing your readers' attention. The <u>middle</u> of the story is about keeping them interested. If the <u>ending</u> comes too easily, without a strong middle, then your reader with think, "That's dull!" If that girl who meets the stray dog brings him home and her parents say, "Oh, goody, let's keep him!" that's not very interesting, is it? If the boy's treasure chest actually turns out to be a box of rusty nails, the reader might say, "Ho hum!"

101

Conflict is the necessary ingredient that helps writers keep their readers' attention in the middle. When a story character wants something, and someone or something gets in the way, that's conflict. The goal of the girl is to keep the stray dog. Conflict comes when the parents say, "No! We don't want a stray dog. We don't want any dog!" The goal of the boy is to find the owner of the treasure chest. Conflict comes when the boy is ambushed by a crew of bandits. "Where did you get that gold coin?" they demand. "That's our money, you thief!" Conflict gets in the way of the character and keeps him from easily reaching his goal.

Read the story of *Alexander and Bucephalus*. Ask yourself, "What conflict in the middle makes the story interesting to read?"

Alexander and Bucephalus

Adapted from James Baldwin, *Fifty Famous Stories Retold*

One day King Philip of Macedon bought a fine horse called Bucephalus. He was a noble animal, and the king paid a very high price for him. But the horse was wild and savage, and no man could mount him, or do anything at all with him.

They tried to whip him, but that only made him worse. At last, the king told his servants to take him away.

"It's a pity to ruin so fine a horse as that," said Alexander, the king's young son. "Those men do not know how to treat him."

"Perhaps you can do better than they," said his father scornfully.

"If you would only give me leave to try," said Alexander, "I could manage this horse better than anyone else."

"And if you fail to do so, what then?" asked Philip.

"I will pay you the price of the horse," said the lad.

While everybody was laughing, Alexander ran up to Bucephalus and turned the horse's head toward the sun. He had noticed that the horse was afraid of his own shadow.

He then spoke gently to the horse, and patted him with his hand. When he had quieted Bucephalus a little, Alexander made a quick spring, and leaped upon the horse's back.

Everybody expected to see the boy killed instantly. But he kept his place, and let the horse run as fast as he would. By and by, when Bucephalus had become tired, Alexander reined him in, and rode back to the place where his father was standing.

All the men who were there shouted when they saw that Alexander had proved himself to be the master of the horse.

The boy leaped to the ground, and his father ran and kissed him. "My son," said the king, "Macedon is too small a place for you. You must seek a larger kingdom that will be worthy of you."

After that, Alexander and Bucephalus were the best of friends. They were said to be always together, for when one of them was seen, the other was sure to be not far away. But the horse would never allow anyone to mount him but his master.

Alexander became the most famous king and warrior that was ever known; and for that reason, he is always called Alexander the Great. Bucephalus carried him through many countries and in many fierce battles, and more than once did he save his master's life.

Tell It Back—Narration

1. **ORAL NARRATION**—Without looking at the myth, tell back *Alexander and Bucephalus* as best as you can remember it using your own words and words from the story. For further practice, you can record your telling back into your favorite recording device and play it afterwards.

   - Keep the events of the story in their proper order.

   ## Here is the first sentence to get you started:

   One day King Philip of Macedon bought a fine horse called Bucephalus.

2. Put the events in order below using *B* for beginning, *M* for middle, and *E* for end.

_____ Everybody expected to see the boy killed instantly. But he kept his place, and let the horse run as fast as he would.

_____ The king paid a very high price for Bucephalus.

_____ "My son," said the king, "Macedon is too small a place for you."

3. **WRITTEN NARRATION**

   a. Write your own sentence to tell what happens at the <u>beginning</u> of the story.

   _____

   _____

   _____

   _____

   b. Write your own sentence to tell what happens in the <u>middle</u> of the story.

   _____

   _____

   _____

   c. Write your own sentence to tell what happens at the <u>end</u> of the story.

   _____

   _____

   _____

Talk About It—

1. What is Alexander's goal in this story? In other words, what does he hope to do?

2. What conflict does Alexander face in this story? What two things are standing in the way of his goal?

3. <u>In the news, a stray dog rescued a woman and her son from a robber who had a knife. The woman and her two-year-old son were strolling away from a playground in Florida when the robber jumped out of the bushes. All of a sudden, a homeless dog snarled and bolted across the playground, attacking the robber and chasing him away.</u> What conflict could be added to the middle of this story to make it even more exciting? What might happen in the end?

4. <u>Also in the news, a boy and his grandfather were walking across a newly plowed field in Sweden when they discovered old silver coins. They dug deeper and found more and more coins. Archaeologists came to the site and carefully dug up the whole area. They found a Viking treasure of 7,000 silver coins from around AD 1200.</u> What conflict could be added to the middle of this story to make it even more exciting? What might happen in the end?

Go Deeper—

1. What kind of narrative do you think *Alexander and Bucephalus* is?
   a. parable
   b. myth
   c. fairy tale
   d. history

2. Because a king and a young prince both admire Bucephalus, the word "noble" probably means:
   a. costly
   b. clever
   c. black
   d. splendid

3. "Perhaps you can do better than they," said his father scornfully. When King Philip tells Alexander, "You can do better," do you think he means it? The word "scornfully" is our clue. What definition comes closest to scornfully?

   a. disrespectfully
   b. honestly
   c. seriously
   d. angrily

4. Who is the dynamic or changing character in this story? How does he change? Use complete sentences. (Hint: It is possible for more than one character in a story to be a dynamic character.)

   _____

   _____

   _____

   _____

   _____

Writing Time—

1. **COPYWORK**—Neatly copy the sentence in the space provided:

   They tried to whip him, but that only made the horse worse.

   _____

   _____

   _____

   _____

   _____

2. **DICTATION**—Your teacher will read a little part of *Alexander and Bucephalus* back to you. Please listen carefully! After your teacher reads once, she will read slowly again and include the punctuation marks. Your task will be to write down the sentences as your teacher reads them one by one.

_____

_____

_____

_____

_____

_____

3. **SENTENCE PLAY**—<u>While everybody was laughing, Alexander ran up to Bucephalus and turned the horse's head toward the sun.</u> Notice that "while" in this sentence serves the same purpose as "as." The sentence would still make sense if you were to say, "As everybody was laughing, Alexander ran up to Bucephalus and turned his head toward the sun." "While" and "as" let us know that two or more things are happening at the same time. What three things are happening at the same time in the sentence about Alexander?

Underline the three things that are happening at the same time in these sentences.

- While the birds played in the sand box, a cat crept up and licked its lips.
- While the rain came down, the kids jumped and danced in the puddles.
- While Fred was swimming, a piranha saw him and bit his toe.

Using these sentences as a model, try to write other sentences with <u>three things</u> happening.

a. While we built a snow fort outside, Mom _____

_____

_____.

b. While the ballerina twirled on stage, the audience _____

_____

_____.

c. While Little Red Riding Hood walked through the dark forest, _____

_____

_____.

d. While _____

_____

_____.

4. COPIOUSNESS

Mark the nouns (3) and verb (1) in the sentence below. Place an *N* over the nouns and *V* over the verb. Replace the nouns and the verb with synonyms, add adjectives, and change the <u>subject</u> to rewrite the simple sentence below. Try to come up with five variations, all keeping nearly the same meaning as the original sentence.

The king paid a high price for the horse.

SUBJECT = The king

Replace nouns and verbs with synonyms.

a. _____

_____

Add adjectives.

b. _____

_____

c. _____

_____

Change the subject.

d. A high price _____

_____

e. The horse _____

_____

Come up with as many <u>variations</u> of the following sentence as you can. Be sure to stay close to the original meaning:

I really don't like gloomy days.

f. _____

_____

g. _____

_____

h. _____

_____

i. _____

_____

j. _____

_____

Lesson 9: *Conflict—The Middle of the Story*

k. _____

_____

5. **AMPLIFICATION WITH DIALOGUE AND DESCRIPTION**—In *The Rich Fool*, we changed the middle and end of the story to create a new story, *The Rich Sage*. This time, let's cut out only the middle part of the story, *Alexander and Bucephalus*, and write it differently. What events would you change? How should the dialogue be different? What would you like to describe in more detail?

- Make sure you add new dialogue.
- Make sure you add a paragraph of description.

Alexander and Bucephalus

Adapted from James Baldwin, *Fifty Famous Stories Retold*

One day King Philip of Macedon bought a fine horse called Bucephalus. He was a noble animal, and the king paid a very high price for him. But the horse was wild and savage, and no man could mount him, or do anything at all with him.

They tried to whip him, but that only made him worse. At last, the king told his servants to take him away.

"It is a pity to ruin so fine a horse as that," said Alexander, the king's young son. "Those men do not know how to treat him."

"Perhaps you can do better than they," said his father scornfully.

"If you would only give me leave to try," said Alexander, "I could manage this horse better than anyone else."

"And if you fail to do so, what then?" asked Philip.

"I will pay you the price of the horse," said the lad.

While everybody was laughing, Alexander ran up to Bucephalus . . .

Now you will need to write your own middle. The following is the part of the story we are cutting out:

[and turned the horse's head toward the sun. He had noticed that the horse was afraid of his own shadow.

He then spoke gently to the horse, and patted him with his hand. When he had quieted Bucephalus a little, Alexander made a quick spring, and leaped upon the horse's back.

Everybody expected to see the boy killed instantly. But he kept his place, and let the horse run as fast as he would. By and by, when Bucephalus had become tired, Alexander reined him in, and rode back to the place where his father was standing.]

Insert your middle section of the story right here:

_____

_____

_____

_____

_____

_____

_____

_____

_____

_____

_____

_____

Lesson 9: Conflict—The Middle of the Story

_____

_____

_____

_____

_____

_____

_____

And the story continues . . .

All the men who were there shouted when they saw that Alexander had proved himself to be the master of the horse.

The boy leaped to the ground, and his father ran and kissed him. "My son," said the king, "Macedon is too small a place for you. You must seek a larger kingdom that will be worthy of you."

After that, Alexander and Bucephalus were the best of friends. They were said to be always together, for when one of them was seen, the other was sure to be not far away. But the horse would never allow anyone to mount him but his master.

Alexander became the most famous king and warrior that was ever known; and for that reason, he is always called Alexander the Great. Bucephalus carried him through many countries and in many fierce battles, and more than once did he save his master's life.

6. **POINT OF VIEW**—*Alexander and Bucephalus* is told by the narrator in the third-person point of view: "he," "she," "it," "they." Tell the story in the <u>first-person point of view</u> ("I," "we") as if you, the storyteller, are Alexander. Or you can tell the story as if you are Philip, the father, or Bucephalus, the horse. If you like, add description and dialogue to amplify the narrative.

_____

_____

_____

_____

_____

_____

_____

_____

_____

_____

_____

_____

_____

_____

_____

_____

Speak It—

Alexander the Great conquered vast areas of the civilized world: Persia, Egypt, and parts of India. And yet his men, the soldiers of Macedon, sometimes became discouraged so far from their homes north of Greece. Before battles, Alexander would give them a rousing speech to encourage them to fight their hardest.

Choose one of the following paragraphs to deliver in class or to record on your favorite recording device. Make your voice strong and brave. The more you practice the passage, the more confident you will sound. Speak loudly, as if you are calling to a vast army of soldiers. Emphasize the most important phrases by speaking them louder or softer than the other "ordinary" words. Some of these phrases are underlined to give you suggestions for phrases to emphasize. Please take a look at the complete elocution instructions on page 129.

Before the Battle of Gaugamela

Who is this great king Darius who enslaves his own men to fight? Who is this king but a king of air? These men do not fight for their homes. They fight because this king tells them they must. When they fight, they will melt away like the air. But we are not here today as slaves. We are here today . . . <u>as Macedonian free men</u>!

Some of you, perhaps myself, will not live to see the sun set over these mountains today, but I say to you what every warrior has known since the beginning of time. Conquer your fear and I promise you, <u>you will conquer death</u>! And when they ask you where you fought so bravely, you will answer, <u>"I was here this day at Gaugamela for the freedom and glory of Greece!"</u>

At the Hyphasis River of India

You and I, gentlemen, have shared the labor and shared the danger, and the rewards are for us all. <u>The conquered territory belongs to you.</u> From your ranks, the governors of it are chosen. Already the greater part of its treasure passes into your hands, and when all Asia is overrun, then indeed I will go further than the mere satisfaction of our ambitions.

<u>The utmost hopes of riches or power</u> which each one of you cherishes <u>will be far surpassed</u>, and whoever wishes to return home will be allowed to go, either with me or without me. <u>I will make those who stay the envy of those who return.</u>

Lesson 9: *Conflict—The Middle of the Story*

Lesson 10

More Practice with Story Middles

What do you like in the middle of your sandwich? Turkey? Ham? Pickles? Cream cheese? Peanut butter and jelly? If you're like me, you enjoy the middle of a sandwich more than the bread on the outside.

The middle of a story is the conflict. Yes, conflict—just as we learned in the previous lesson! No story is enjoyable when the main character too easily reaches his goals. Expert storytellers will put obstacles in the way of the main character, and readers enjoy seeing how the character will overcome those obstacles.

Look back at every story in this book and you will see conflict. In *The Prodigal Son*, the young man wants to live high on the hog, but ends up feeding hogs and longing for home. In *Athena Defeats Poseidon*, Athena must struggle with the god of the sea to win the naming contest for the city. In *Athena and Arachne*, a mortal woman vies with a goddess to win a weaving contest. In *The Brave 300*, the Spartans fight a much more numerous foe. And so on.

We are going to look at several story <u>beginnings</u> and <u>endings</u>. It will be your job to supply the middles. Use dialogue, description, and conflict to make a lively middle for your reader to enjoy. The middle should make sense, both with the beginning and with the end. Make sure to look ahead to the ending so that you know where the middle of your story needs to go.

If you draw a blank for conflict in the middle, ask your teacher for help. Together you can brainstorm some fun ideas.

The Johnny-Cake

Adapted from the English tale by Joseph Jacobs
(Note: A johnnycake is a fried cornmeal pancake.)

Once upon a time, there was an old man, and an old woman, and a little boy. One morning, the old woman made a johnny-cake and put it in the oven to bake.

"You watch the johnny-cake while your father and I go out to work in the garden," the old woman told the boy.

So the old man and the old woman went out and began to hoe potatoes and left the little boy to tend the oven. But he didn't watch it all the time. All of a sudden, he heard a noise, and he looked up and the oven door popped open. Out of the oven jumped Johnny-Cake, and he went rolling along end-over-end toward the open door of the house.

The little boy ran to shut the door, but Johnny-Cake was too quick for him. Johnny-Cake rolled through the door, down the steps, and out into the road long before the little boy could catch him. The little boy ran after him as fast as he could, crying out to his father and mother, who heard the uproar and threw down their hoes and gave chase, too. But Johnny-Cake outran all three a long way, and he was soon out of sight. The father, mother, and son had to sit down, all out of breath, on a bank to rest.

_____

_____

_____

_____

_____

_____

_____

_____

_____

_____

_____

_____

Lesson 10: More Practice with Story Middles

_____

_____

_____

_____

_____

_____

_____

_____

_____

_____

_____

_____

_____

_____

_____

_____

_____

And the story continues . . .

And the fox snapped up the johnny-cake in his sharp teeth and gulped him down.

The Sausage

A folktale of Sweden

There was once a poor old lady who was granted three wishes by a fairy queen. "Three wishes!" the old lady exclaimed with delight, and she began to think what she should wish for. She expected her husband back soon, and she thought it would be best to wait until he came home and could have a say in the matter. But the least they could wish for must be a fine big farm—the best in the parish, and a box full of money, and just fancy how happy and comfortable they would be then, for they had worked so hard all their days! Ah, yes, then the neighbors would have something to wonder at, for you may guess how they would stare at all the fine things she would have.

But now that they would soon be so rich, it was really a shame that there should be nothing but some blue, sour milk and some hard crusts of bread in the cupboard for her husband when he came home tired and weary, he who was fond of hot food. She had just been to her neighbor's and there she had seen a fine big sausage, which the neighbors were going to have for supper.

"Ah, deary me, I wish I had that sausage here!" sighed the old lady, and the next moment, a big sausage lay on the table right before her.

She was just going to put it in the pan when her husband came in.

"Husband, husband!" cried the Old Lady. "It's all over with our troubles and hard work now. I lent my brewing pan to a fine woman, and when she brought it back, she said she was a fairy queen and promised we could have three wishes. And now you must help me to wish for something really good, for you're so clever at hitting upon the right thing—and it's all true, for just look at the sausage, which I got the moment I wished for it!"

"What do you mean, you silly old lady?" shouted the husband, who became angry. "Have you been wishing for such a paltry thing as a sausage, when you might have had anything you liked in the world?"

Lesson 10: *More Practice with Story Middles*

_____

_____

_____

_____

_____

_____

_____

_____

_____

_____

And the story continues...

And in the end, the old couple were just as poor as ever.

Samba the Coward

Adapted from an African tale by Andrew Lang

In a great country far away south, through which flows the river Nile, there lived a king who had an only child called Samba.

Now, from the time that Samba could walk, he showed signs of being afraid of everything, and as he grew bigger, he became more and more frightened. At first his father's friends made light of it, and said to each other: "It is strange to see a boy of our race running into a hut at the trumpeting of an elephant, and trembling with fear if a lion cub half his size comes near him; but, after all, he is only a baby, and when he is older, he will be as brave as the rest."

"Yes, he is only a baby," answered the king, who overheard them. "It will be all right by-and-by." But, somehow, the king sighed as he said it, and the men looked at him and made no reply.

The years passed away, and Samba had become a tall and strong youth. He was good-natured and pleasant, and was liked by all, and if during his father's hunting parties, he was seldom to be seen in any place of danger, he was too great a favorite for much to be said.

At long last, the celebration of Samba's passage into manhood was nearing, and the people said, "When the king holds the feast and declares Samba to be his heir, he will cease to be a child." Then, on the day of the ceremony, their hearts beat gladly, and they cried to each other: "It is Samba, Samba, whose chin is above the heads of other men, who will defend us against the tribes of the robbers!"

Not many weeks after, the dwellers in the village awoke to find that during the night their herds had been driven away, and their herdsmen carried off into slavery by their enemies. Now was the time for Samba to show the brave spirit that had come to him with his manhood, and to ride forth at the head of the warriors of his race. But Samba could nowhere be found, and a party of the avengers went on their way without him.

It was many days later before Samba came back, with his head held high, and a tale of a lion, which he had tracked to its lair and killed, at the risk of his own life. A little while earlier his people would have welcomed his story, and believed it all, but now it was too late.

"Samba the Coward," cried a voice from the crowd; and the name stuck to him, even the very children shouted it at him, and his father did not spare him. At length Samba could bear it no longer, and he made up his mind to leave his own land for another where peace had reigned since the memory of man. So, early next morning, he slipped out to the king's stables, and choosing the quietest horse he could find, he rode away northwards.

_____

_____

Lesson 10: More Practice with Story Middles

_____

_____

_____

_____

_____

_____

_____

_____

_____

_____

_____

_____

_____

_____

And the story continues . . .

When he returned to his village, Samba was no longer the coward, the terrified, the fraidy cat—he was every inch the warrior. Everyone said it was a miracle, but Samba himself knew the secret of his bravery.

Elocution Instructions

Whether you are reciting a poem or reading a story out loud, you want to speak in such a way that the audience can hear you "loud and clear." The art of speaking skillfully is known as elocution. So, what goes into proper elocution?

First of all, you should make sure you are <u>pronouncing all of your words clearly</u>. This means you are making each word sharp and crisp instead of blending them together and mumbling. You want to say, "To be or not to be, that is the question," with each word separate from the next. You don't want to say, "Tobeornottobethatis-thequestion."

Secondly, <u>good posture</u> is very important for speaking loudly enough. You can't breathe very well if you are slouched over. Stand up straight and tall, square your shoulders and look at your audience. <u>Look directly into their eyes.</u> This will help your listeners know that you are a confident speaker. They will enjoy your recitation more when they see how confident you are.

Finally, don't speak too quickly. It's hard to understand a recitation that blasts off like a rocket ship. You will want to <u>speak at a good pace</u> and pause every now and then to let your words sink in.

You will delight to your listeners if you can stand up straight, look into their eyes, and speak loud and clear at just the right pace.

Glossary of Words in This Book

New Concepts

Conflict—a clash between people or ideas

Dialogue—a conversation between two or more people

Dynamic character—a character who changes in the course of a narrative

Epitaph—words inscribed on a grave marker

Fable—a short story that teaches a simple moral lesson, usually with talking animals

Fairy tale—a fanciful story for children, usually with magical people or creatures

Fiction—any imaginative story

History—a narrative of actual events

Main idea—the most important thought in a story or speech; what the story or speech is all about

Monologue—a long speech by one person or character

Myth—an ancient story not based on actual events, with gods, goddesses, and heroes

Narrative—all forms of story, from fairy tale, to history, to myths, to parables, to fables

Parable—a short story that teaches a moral lesson, always true to life

Proper noun—noun that names a specific person, place, thing, or idea

Synonym—a word that has nearly the same meaning as another word

Vocabulary Builder

Countenance (noun)—the face

Devour (verb)—to eat greedily

Mortal (adjective)—anyone or anything that will die

Immortal (adjective)—anyone or anything that will not die

Loom (noun)—a wooden frame used to weave cloth

Prodigal—wasteful (adjective)/a wasteful person (noun)

Resolve (verb)—to clear up or solve; to make a firm decision

Sage (noun)—a wise person

Shuttle (noun)—a tool used by weavers to pull thread through other threads

Stomach (verb)—to put up with; to tolerate

Token (noun)—a sign or proof of something

Tyrant (noun)—a harsh, cruel, or unfair ruler

Another Good-bye—

Yes, it's time to say good-bye once again. Before we part company, let's take a moment to consider what you've learned.

You've learned that narratives are stories and that the world is full of all sorts of them: fables, fairy tales, myths, histories, parables, and so on. Nearly all narratives contain a beginning, a middle, and an end, as well as characters. The best narratives have conflict in the middle. They also contain colorful dialogue, lively characters, and description.

But wait, there's more! You've learned to recognize certain parts of speech: nouns, adjectives, and verbs. A noun is a person, place, thing, or idea. An adjective describes a noun to help us see it more clearly. A verb is often the action word of a sentence. If you recognize these types of words, you can improve your skills in building happier, stronger, more sparkling sentences. Don't forget that most words—nouns, adjectives, and verbs included—have synonyms. Synonyms are words that mean nearly the same thing as another word. They are extremely helpful in learning to write copiously.

You are also learning to speak with better elocution, which is the art of speaking skillfully. As a speaker you are standing up straight and tall, looking into the eyes of your audience, and speaking loud and clear.

When we meet again in the next book,

Writing & Rhetoric: Narrative II, we will take everything we learned in this book and create our own narratives from scratch. You, my dear, will be an author! You will create your own make-believe world and what could be more fun than that?

Good-bye and au revoir, auf Wiedersehen, *zai jian*, *sayonara*, shalom, adios, *kwaheri*, and *do svidaniya*!

Notes

Notes

Notes

Notes